Fuentes de Oñoro

Wellington's liberation of Portugal

Campaign • 99

Fuentes de Oñoro

Wellington's liberation of Portugal

René Chartrand • Illustrated by Patrice Courcelle

Series editor Lee Johnson • Consultant editor David G Chandler

First published in Great Britain in 2002 by Osprey Publishing, Elms Court, Chapel Way, Botley, Oxford OX2 9LP, United Kingdom.
Email: info@ospreypublishing.com

ISBN 1 84176 311 X

Editor: Lee Johnson
Design: The Black Spot
Index by Alan Rutter
Maps by The Map Studio
3D bird's eye views by Encompass Graphics
Battlescene artwork by Patrice Courcelle
Originated by Magnet Harlequin, Uxbridge, UK
Printed in China through World Print Ltd.

02 03 04 05 06   10 9 8 7 6 5 4 3 2 1

For a catalogue of all books published by Osprey Military and Aviation please contact:

The Marketing Manager, Osprey Direct UK, PO Box 140,
Wellingborough, Northants, NN8 4ZA, United Kingdom.
Email: info@ospreydirect.co.uk

The Marketing Manager, Osprey Direct USA,
c/o Motorbooks International, PO Box 1,
Osceola, WI 54020-0001, USA.
Email: info@ospreydirectusa.com

www.ospreypublishing.com

KEY TO MILITARY SYMBOLS

Dedication

To the memory of Manuel Veludo Coelho

Acknowledgements

In Portugal, I have again had considerable assistance from Dr. Sergio Veludo Coelho and Mr. Pedro de Brito of Porto who kindly gave access to his fine collection. The Museu Militar do Porto (Porto Military Museum) was most helpful as were the Archivo Historico Militar in Lisbon. In Great Britain, I am especially grateful to the staff at the Public Records Office at Kew. Patrice Courcelle skilfully illustrated key events of the campaign. All this material could never have come together in a handsome book without the fine editorial work of Lee Johnson and Marcus Cowper's coordination at Osprey. To one and all, please accept my heartfelt expression of deepest gratitude.

Author's Note

The battle of Fuentes de Oñoro, fought on 3 and 5 May 1811, is rightly regarded as one of the great British victories of the Peninsular War. It was the engagement that put an end to the third French invasion of Portugal. It was also the most destructive invasion ever suffered by that country, with hundreds of thousands of Portuguese civilians left ruined and homeless besides the thousands killed by rampaging French troops. This invasion, which had started in the summer of 1810, reached its climax in the battle of Bussaco (see Campaign 97 *Bussaco 1810*) and was halted at the Lines of Torres Vedras. From there, the French army would retreat before the amazingly resilient, efficient and nearly always outnumbered Anglo-Portuguese army, a road that ended in the small Spanish border village of Fuentes de Oñoro. By the end of the battle, Marshal Masséna, once one of France's finest generals, was a totally vanquished man, never to lead an army again. It had been a close call for his opponent, Wellington, but he was now confirmed as an outstanding tactician and one of Europe's great captains.

The spelling of Portuguese words generally follows the adaptations that have long been prevalent in British and American military and historical publications, in particular as expressed by Oxford Professor Sir Charles Oman in his *History of the Peninsular War*.

The following abbreviations are used throughout the footnotes: Public Records Office (Kew, UK) – PRO; Audit Office – AO; Foreign Office – FO; War Office – WO.

Artist's note

Readers may care to note that the original paintings from which the colour plates in this book were prepared are available for private sale. All reproduction copyright whatsoever is retained by the Publishers. All enquiries should be addressed to:

Patrice Courcelle
33 Avenue des Vallons
1410 Waterloo,
Belgium

The Publishers regret that they can enter into no correspondence upon this matter.

CONTENTS

THE PENINSULA, OCTOBER 1810

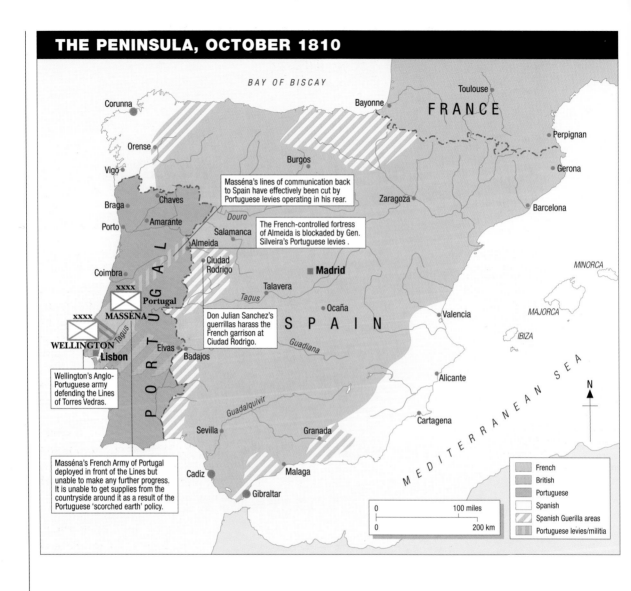

BAY OF BISCAY

Corunna

Orense

Vigo

Braga

Porto

Chaves

Amarante

PORTUGAL

Coimbra

Portugal

MASSENA

WELLINGTON

Lisbon

Elvas

Badajos

Toulouse

Bayonne

FRANCE

Perpignan

Gerona

Barcelona

Burgos

Zaragoza

Salamanca

Almeida

Ciudad Rodrigo

Madrid

Talavera

Douro

Tagus

Ocaña

Valencia

Tagus

Guadiana

Sevilla

Granada

Cadiz

Malaga

Gibraltar

Alicante

Cartagena

SPAIN

Guadalquivir

MINORCA

MAJORCA

IBIZA

MEDITERRANEAN SEA

Masséna's lines of communication back to Spain have effectively been cut by Portuguese levies operating in his rear.

The French-controlled fortress of Almeida is blockaded by Gen. Silveira's Portuguese levies .

Don Julian Sanchez's guerrillas harass the French garrison at Ciudad Rodrigo.

Wellington's Anglo-Portuguese army defending the Lines of Torres Vedras.

Masséna's French Army of Portugal deployed in front of the Lines but unable to make any further progress. It is unable to get supplies from the countryside around it as a result of the Portuguese 'scorched earth' policy.

N

0	100 miles
0	200 km

	French
	British
	Portuguese
	Spanish
	Spanish Guerilla areas
	Portuguese levies/militia

ORIGINS OF THE CAMPAIGN

In October 1810, the outlook appeared optimistic for Napoleon I, Emperor of the French. The last 20 years of his life had been truly amazing: in 1790, he was an obscure young subaltern officer in the French artillery who disliked France and yearned to liberate his native Corsica. Five years later, he was a general in the French army leading his troops to victory in Italy; in 1800, he was the most important of the three consuls that governed France; by 1805, he had been crowned emperor and had vanquished Austria; by 1810, Prussia and Russia had joined Austria in defeat and the French imperial eagles were unchallenged from France to Poland. Napoleon had even succeeded in coaxing the reluctant Pope to grant him a divorce from the barren Empress Joséphine. This allowed him to marry young Princess Marie-Louise of Austria in order to bear an heir to the imperial throne as well as to seal a pan-European alliance. On 27 March 1811, Empress Marie-Louise gave birth to a sturdy baby boy. Napoleon was overjoyed. The baby was given the name of Napoleon and made King of Rome. A successor to the imperial throne seemed assured.

On one occasion, Napoleon had surprised his mother, who was busy with her investment bankers, making fun of her and saying that she was past such worries as the Bonapartes ruled Europe and all its riches. Letitia Buonaparte, who had known poverty and want in her younger years, answered that such confidence was foolish, that one never knew what could happen or lay ahead so that it was always wise to save for rainy days. The emperor shrugged and left.[1]

In some ways, the first of those rainy days for Napoleon's imperial regime had come on 11 October 1810 in far-away Portugal. That day, the French cavalrymen pursuing the retreating Anglo-Portuguese army reached 'the lines' which appeared to block, at least temporarily, the advance of Marshal Masséna and his French 'Army of Portugal'. They also constituted an irritating delay to Masséna's triumphant entry into Lisbon after months of difficult campaigning. At first, these lines were thought to be some last minute field works thrown up by Wellington's retreating army, but they were strangely uniform in construction. General of Division Louis-Pierre Montbrun, the French cavalry commander on the spot, ordered parties of scouts to reconnoitre. Patrol after patrol of dumbfounded cavalrymen galloped back to Montbrun and his staff officers

Napoleon meets Francis II, Emperor of Austria, following the great French victory at Austerlitz on 2 December 1805. From then on, Napoleon saw himself more as emperor of Europe. (Print after Gros)

reporting that the network of cleverly sited fortifications extended along the hills as far as they could see in either direction. In addition, far from being rough, hastily erected earthworks, some appeared to be major forts bristling with cannon and full of soldiers.

What these scouts had in fact encountered were the soon-to-be-famous Lines of Torres Vedras, one of the most sophisticated integrated defence systems yet devised. Although not clear at the time, the French army had reached its high water mark in the peninsula.

Watching the progress of the French armies in Spain and Portugal on a map in Paris, it must have seemed to Napoleon and his senior officers that – at last – they were about to witness the final act of the war in the Iberian peninsula. Soon, the couriers from Masséna's army would announce the embarkation of the British army evacuating the Portuguese capital and its occupation by the French army. With the only major force capable of resisting the French out of the way, other opposition in Spain and Portugal would ultimately collapse.

Indeed from the British viewpoint the situation in Portugal was far from cheerful in 1810. Years after the war, Sir John Colborne, the future Lord Seaton, who had served within Wellington's army at the time, skilfully summed it up: *Between the months of February and August, 1810, the affairs of the Peninsula appeared almost hopeless. Andalusia had quietly submitted* [to the French]. *The last large army of the Spaniards had been dispersed. Seville was occupied … Masséna had taken Ciudad Rodrigo, was besieging Almeida, and preparing to march on Lisbon through Beira with an army of about 70,000* [men]. *Lord Wellington manoeuvred in Beira and in the Alemtejo with an army of about 50,000 English and Portuguese. He had to contend against a Ministry frightened at the risk of exposing a British army and while he, unmoved by their fears, was carrying into execution one of the most scientific campaigns of those days, the British Ministers were thinking of preparations for embarking the troops … He also had to contend against another faction of the Portuguese Government that imagined he was withdrawing. As soon as it became know that his intention was to retire ultimately on Lisbon, the Bishop of Porto drew up a strong remonstrance, in which he threatened that the Portuguese troops should be withdrawn from Lord Wellington's command if he did not defend the frontier.*

In the event, the fortress of Almeida was destroyed in a disastrous explosion and, full of confidence, the French swept into Portugal until they reached Bussaco. There, on 27 September 1810, Wellington's Allied army gave the French a severe rebuke, which dampened their morale while raising the hopes of the British and Portuguese. Colborne wrote his sister Alethea two days later that 'this action very much changed the appearance of affairs in Portugal. The Portuguese troops have established their character … They behaved in a most gallant manner,

The marriage of Napoleon to Marie-Louise of Austria celebrated at the Louvre in Paris on 2 April 1810. (Print after Rouget)

Napoleon and Marie-Louise show their baby boy to the imperial court in March 1811. He had already been named King of Rome and heir to Napoleon's empire. (Print after Rouget)

and full as well as the British.'[2] As can be seen from contemporary correspondence, including that of King George III, the performance of the Portuguese was a great encouragement to the British. The front opened against the French in the Peninsula had seemed full of promise with the massive risings in Spain and Portugal in 1808 against Napoleon's rule. Two years later, the picture seemed very gloomy to anyone in Britain. As heroic as the Spanish could be, their hopelessly inefficient regular armies had been repeatedly crushed, and what Spanish government that remained seemed quite hostile to the British – to be fair, Britain was Spain's ancient enemy – and certainly deeply suspicious of Britain's motives. Even rumours of some partial British control of troops or territory could create a major diplomatic crisis between Spain and Britain.

So there remained only Portugal, the small kingdom and steadfast ally of Britain since the Middle Ages. The Portuguese had taken a very different approach from their Iberian neighbour. Prince Regent Joao VI had left Lisbon in November 1807, establishing his court in Rio de Janeiro, Brazil, Portugal's large and very prosperous colony. With regard to their armed forces, the practical and pragmatic Portuguese were more interested in efficiency than in the politics of pride, and they readily accommodated hundreds of British officers to transform their army into a first-class fighting force – even accepting a British officer, Beresford, as their marshal and thus most senior officer. The Portuguese people made enormous personal sacrifices to win Allied victories and oust the French from their country. All this was not achieved without difficulty, but by late 1810 the incredible task was basically complete: the country had been laid waste largely by its own inhabitants, making life all but impossible for the ever-hungry French invaders. At the same time, under the watchful eye of Viscount Wellington, the Allied army of British and Portuguese troops, although still small, was evolving into one of the best fighting forces in Europe. Hence Colonel Colborne's optimism.

---

1 Napoleon's mother was right and, after the imperial regime fell in 1814–15, she used the fortune saved to help those members of the family in want. For Napoleon's youth, see the *Osprey Military Journal*, Volume 2, issues 4 and 5.

2 Quoted in G.C. Moore Smith, *The Life of John Colborne, Field Marshal Lord Seaton* (London, 1903), pp. 141, 143–144.

CHRONOLOGY

1809

April, Wellington appointed to command in Portugal, as commander-in-chief of the British and Portuguese forces.

Late October, Lines of Torres Vedras started north of Lisbon.

1810

17 April, Marshal Masséna appointed by Napoleon to conquer Portugal.

26 August, Disastrous explosion destroys the fortress of Almeida; French army pours into Portugal.

27 September, Battle of Bussaco.

11 October, French reach the Lines of Torres Vedras.

15–18 November, French fall back to Santarem.

26 December, Elements of the French 9th Corps reach Masséna's army.

1811

Early March, General retreat of the French from Santarem.

12–16 March, Clashes at Redinha, Casal Novo and Foz d'Aronce.

23 March, Marshal Ney is dismissed by Masséna and leaves Portugal.

5 April, Clash at Sabugal.

3–5 May, Battle of Fuentes de Oñoro.

10–11 May, French garrison of Almeida slips through British lines.

11 May, Marshal Marmont replaces Marshal Masséna.

OPPOSING PLANS

General of Division Michel Clarapède (1772–1842). Clarapède led a division of the 9th Corps which was heavily engaged at Fuentes de Oñoro on 5 May 1811.

THE FRENCH

As they approached Lisbon after the battle of Bussaco and their sacking of Coimbra, the French plan was simple enough. They would sweep everything before them as they had previously, except that next time they met the Anglo-Portuguese troops would not have a strong defensive position from which to maul the French army as at Bussaco. Thus, although shaken by their experience at Bussaco, the French were confident that the British troops would have no choice but to embark on their ships and leave Lisbon. Perhaps here and there a strong redoubt might have to be besieged but, in the long run, Lisbon would fall.

Once the formidable Lines of Torres Vedras were reached, the plan for the leisurely capture of Lisbon vaporised. Masséna and his generals had no inkling of the existence of these fortifications and had never planned for anything of the sort. The probe at Sobral and other skirmishes confirmed the extraordinary strength and extent of this network. From then on, there was no French plan, only increasingly desperate improvisation in a worsening situation. Thus was the retreat of the starving army to Santarem brought about, and thus the retreat to the Spanish border. While it might be argued that the battle of Fuentes de Oñoro occurred because Masséna wanted to maintain a foothold in Portugal to allow a later invasion, this was more wishful thinking than a genuine plan.

THE ANGLO-PORTUGUESE

General of Division Louis-Pierre Montbrun (1770–1812), commander of the cavalry reserve of Masséna's army.

The aim of the British and the Portuguese was to inflict as much damage as possible on the French invasion army while keeping their own fighting capacity as intact as possible. Even while Wellington's Anglo-Portuguese army was fighting to delay the French in the north, the country mobilised to build the Lines of Torres Vedras according to Wellington's far-sighted defence plan of the autumn of 1809. When the French eventually reached the lines it would require considerable efforts to pierce the defences. Another part of the plan was a 'scorched earth' policy by the Portuguese to leave as little as possible to the French troops, who were used to living off the land. In the event, the French army could not ultimately sustain itself before the Lines and had to retreat to Santarem to survive. The next step would be for Wellington's Allied army to pursue them to Spain and, if the opportunity arose, to bring on a general engagement – an opportunity that would come at the small dusty village of Fuentes de Oñoro.

OPPOSING LEADERS

THE FRENCH

Marshal André Masséna, Duke of Rivoli, Prince of Essling (1756–1817).
Masséna served in the French infantry from 1775 to 1789 when he left
the service. He rejoined the army in 1792 and was a major-general by
1793. He campaigned with Bonaparte in Italy and was truly outstanding
in the Swiss campaign of 1799–1800, winning the battle of Zurich against
the Austrians and Russians. A marshal in 1804, esteemed by Napoleon,
Masséna also had a taste for looting. His strategic and tactical talents
were instinctive as he never pursued theoretical studies since he disliked
reading. Following the Austrian campaign of 1809, Napoleon had
entrusted the conquest of Portugal to Masséna, who was then considered
one of his best marshals and was nicknamed *l'enfant chéri de la victoire* (the
cherished child of victory) by the French. Nevertheless, victory eluded
him as he marched deeper and deeper into Portugal. The battle of
Bussaco, fought on 27 September 1810 (see Campaign 97 *Bussaco 1810*),
was a rude surprise for the overconfident French army. Masséna reacted
quickly and managed to outflank the Anglo-Portuguese army, something
which his opponent had foreseen as a whole strategy had been
developed with the Lines of Torres Vedras as a bulwark. When faced with
this new and unforeseen obstacle, Masséna did not bother with a
personal reconnaissance for some days, displaying a tired, *laissez-faire*
attitude that seems to have afflicted him throughout the campaign.
Wellington was on his guard nevertheless as he respected Masséna as a
'sly old fox' of a tactician, which he certainly demonstrated at Fuentes de
Oñoro. Replaced by Marshal Marmont on 11 May, Masséna was never
again entrusted with senior commands.

Marshal Michel Ney, Duke of Elchingen (1769–1815). Originally a law
clerk, Ney joined the hussars in 1788 as a private, was a brigadier-general
by 1794 and marshal in 1804. Temperamental and occasionally an
extraordinary tactician, he was outstanding in action and a superb leader
of men in battle. He commanded the 6th Corps during the 1810–1811
Portuguese campaign but detested Masséna, who finally relieved him
from duty in March 1811, much to the chagrin of the men. Napoleon
later gave Ney other corps commands and named him Prince of the
Moskova for his outstanding conduct in Russia. Following the abdication
of Napoleon in 1814, Ney rallied to the Royalist Government. When
Napoleon returned from Elba in the spring of 1815, Ney at first
promised King Louis XVIII he would capture Napoleon but, like so
many of his soldiers, he rejoined the emperor instead. He fought with
great bravery at Waterloo, charging with the French cavalry. Accused of
treason by the royal government following Napoleon's final exile, Ney

TOP **Marshal André Masséna,
Duke of Rivoli, Prince of Essling
(1756–1817). Print after a c.1800
portrait taken when he was at
the peak of his tactical abilities.**

ABOVE **Marshal André Masséna,
Duke of Rivoli, Prince of Essling
(1756–1817). Print after a c.1808
portrait by Fontaine.**

Marshal Michel Ney, Duke of Elchingen (1769–1815). Ney, who led the 6th Corps of Masséna's army, was one the most valiant battlefield commanders of the imperial army. However, the two men could not get along and Masséna dismissed Ney from his command in March 1811. (Print after Meissonier)

General Andoche Junot, Duke of Abrantes (1771–1813). He commanded the 8th Corps of Masséna's army.

was executed by firing squad in the moat of Vincennes castle. He remained 'the bravest of the brave', as Napoleon once called him, to the end. His last words were to the soldiers of his firing squad: 'aim at the heart, that is where brave men should be hit!'

General Jean-Louis Reynier (1771–1814) was a Swiss who joined the French army in 1792 and rose to general in 1795 thanks to his exceptional efficiency. Although a strict disciplinarian Reynier was humane, brave and honest but also cold and taciturn. As a result, he was not well liked by his troops. After the 1810–1811 campaign, he went on to serve in Russia in 1812 and Germany the following year.

General Andoche Junot, Duke of Abrantes (1771–1813), was one of Napoleon's closest friends during his early career. He campaigned in Italy in the 1790s and fought at Austerlitz. He was a good soldier if not an outstanding general. Previously ambassador to Portugal, he and his men managed to occupy the country without resistance in November 1807, being named Duke of Abrantes by Napoleon as a result. However, he was expelled once the British landed in August 1808. Junot was given command of the 8th Army Corps for the 1810–1811 campaign, but his corps was usually held in reserve. He later commanded it in Russia.

General Jean-Baptiste Drouet D'Erlon commanded the 9th Corps sent to reinforce Masséna. His corps made a series of courageous attacks in an attempt to secure the village of Fuentes de Oñoro on 5 May 1811 but to no avail. Drouet campaigned until the final battle at Toulouse in 1814 and fought at Waterloo in 1815.

Jean-Baptiste-Maurice Loison (1771–1816) rose through the ranks by his sheer bravery in numerous campaigns. Wounded several times, he lost an arm in combat. He came to Portugal with Junot as a general of division in late 1807 and was a redoubtable opponent who would immediately pounce on his enemy's mistakes. There was a darker side to Loison, however. He was a cruel individual who believed that only wanton violence, especially against the weak and defenceless, would subdue the Portuguese. He replaced Marshal Ney in command of the 6th Corps but did not have the tactical ability of his predecessor. After serving in Portugal and Spain, he fought with distinction in Russia in 1812, in Germany in 1813 and held Hamburg in 1814. He retired as a much-decorated, hard-fighting soldier.

Marshal Jean-Baptiste Bessières, Duke of Istria (1766–1813), was the commander of the Imperial Guard cavalry and an intelligent officer who cared for his men. On 8 January 1811 Napoleon regrouped several commands in northern Spain and named Bessières commander of the 70,000-man 'Army of the North', which included units from the Imperial Guard. Masséna accused him, perhaps with some justification, of failing to assist him during the battle of Fuentes de Oñoro. He was killed in action in Germany in early 1813.

Marshal Auguste Frédéric Marmont, Duke of Ragusa (1774–1852), replaced Masséna in command of the 'Army of Portugal' in May,

Marshal Jean-Baptiste Bessières, Duke of Istria (1766–1813), Colonel-General of the cavalry of the Imperial Guard and commander of the French Army of the North in Spain. His role in the battle of Fuentes de Oñoro on 5 May 1811 was nebulous to say the least. (Print after JOB)

Lieutenant-General Arthur Wellesley, Viscount Wellington (1769–1852), commander in chief of the Allied forces in 1810. He was appointed to command the British forces in Portugal in April 1809 and appointed marshal-general of the Portuguese army on 6 July. He was created a peer with the title of Viscount Wellington on 26 August 1809. In this print after Thomas Lawrence's 1814 portrait, Wellington is shown in his usual dress on campaign, a frock coat and a cape if the weather got chilly.

reorganised it into a fearsome force, and frequently outmanoeuvred Wellington until defeated at Salamanca in 1812, where he was badly wounded. He later campaigned in Germany and France during 1813–1814 until, discouraged, he went over to the Allies.

THE BRITISH

Sir Arthur Wellesley, Viscount Wellington (1769–1852). The future Duke of Wellington campaigned in Holland during 1794–1795, was in India from 1796, where he won much distinction for his victories over the Mahrattas at Assaye and Argaun in 1803. Back in England in 1806, he led a brigade at Copenhagen in 1807. Promoted to lieutenant-general, he was given command of the British troops landing in Portugal in July 1808. He performed brilliantly during August beating the French at Roliça and Vimeiro. He was appointed marshal-general of the Portuguese forces and thus became the commander-in-chief of the Allied army on 29 April 1809. Wellington retook Porto from Marshal Soult in April 1809 and beat Marshal Victor at Talavera on 27 August confirming his talents as a general. The invasion of Portugal in 1810 put a great strain on Wellington. Sir John Colborne's statement that the 'responsibility of repelling the invasion rested on the shoulders of Lord Wellington' was certainly true and a heavy burden it must have been. But, tireless worker though he was, he knew how to relax and was often out hunting with the pack of hounds he kept, even on campaign. Following the battle of Fuentes de Oñoro in May 1811, Wellington campaigned successfully in Spain in 1812–1813 and was in southern France by 1814. His victory over Napoleon at Waterloo on 18 June 1815 won him an honoured place in the pantheon of history's great generals. He later became commander-in-chief of the British army and prime minister.

Major-General Thomas Picton (1758–1815) campaigned in the West Indies and was governor of Trinidad until 1806 when he returned to England. In early 1810, Picton was sent to Portugal at Wellington's request and appointed to command the 3rd Division. Picton's performance during the 1810–1811 campaign in Portugal was outstanding. His 3rd Division was heavily engaged in the battle of Bussaco, often forming the rearguard in the subsequent retreat to Torres Vedras. With the Light Division, Picton's Division was the spearhead of Wellington's army and performed brilliantly in the pursuit of the French army to the Spanish border. Picton could always be depended upon to put the pressure on the enemy. He had a very good tactical eye on the battlefield, loved his men as well as roundly cursing them on numerous occasions. They in turn, respected and admired their general for his rough yet fatherly ways. He went on to distinguished service during the rest of the Peninsular War but was killed at Waterloo.

A good many other field officers served ably during the campaign. Wellington was very relieved to see **Brigadier-General Robert Craufurd**, the talented commander of his Light Division, return from leave in England in the nick of time for the battle of Fuentes de Oñoro. A good thing too, as the division was, typically, heavily engaged in holding the

Allied southern flank. It was a welcome relief as its interim commander, **Sir William Erskine**, 'generally understood to be a madman' according to Wellington, might not have done as well, bearing in mind his dubious performance at Sabugal.[3] **Stapleton Cotton** (1773–1865) was the cavalry 'beau sabreur' general of the British forces in Portugal. He did not have many troopers to counter the masses of French cavalry, but he made the most of those he did have, making especially good use of his light cavalry, which seemed to be everywhere during the campaign. **Major-General Rowland Hill** was Wellington's most trusted independent corps commander at the Lines of Torres Vedras and later in eastern Portugal, but he became ill with malaria at the end of 1810. **Richard Fletcher** of the Royal Engineers did outstanding work supervising the building of the lines, although the contribution of the Portuguese to their construction was more significant than previously thought by British historians, as outlined below.

THE PORTUGUESE AND SPANISH

Marshal William Carr Beresford (1768–1854) was the commander-in-chief of the Portuguese army from 1809 until 1820, and he was one of the officers upon whom Wellington depended most for counsel and support. Beresford was commissioned in 1785 and saw much action in the Mediterranean, India, Egypt, the Cape of Good Hope and Buenos Aires. In late 1807, as Portugal was being invaded by the French, Beresford commanded a British force that occupied Madeira for fear that the French might use it as a naval base. While there, Beresford was attracted to Lusitanian culture and learned to speak Portuguese which he improved when he came to Portugal itself with the rank of major-general in the latter part of 1808, and was with Sir John Moore during the retreat to Corunna. Recognised for his special talents in organisation and administration, he was appointed marshal of the Portuguese army on 7 March 1809 and relentlessly went to work reorganising it into one of the most efficient forces of the Napoleonic wars. From January to June 1811, Beresford replaced an ailing Rowland Hill at the command of the Anglo-Portuguese troops east of the Tagus River which led him into western Spain. On 16 May 1811, he won the hard-fought battle of Albuera against Marshal Soult, but Beresford was not an outstanding tactician and it was a close call. He went on to serve with Wellington in Spain and southern France.

The most notable Portuguese general during the campaign was **Major-General Francisco de Silveira** who managed to keep the pressure on Masséna's lines of communications in northern Portugal, cutting them almost totally between mid-September and mid-November 1810 thanks to his blockade of Almeida. He knew his forces, consisting mainly of militia and Ordenanza levies from northeastern Portugal, could not hope to stand against the French army. Once Drouet's 9th Corps arrived as reinforcements for Masséna, his purpose was to tie down as much of it as possible, defending the lines of communication, and in this he was most successful. He was made Count of Amarante in 1812 by Prince Regent Joao VI for his services. **Lieutenant-General Manuel Pinto Bacelar** commanded the forces, again mostly levies, in the northwest and

TOP **Major-General Thomas Picton (1758–1815) commanded the 3rd Division in the Anglo-Portuguese army. It saw action on 3 May and was heavily engaged on 5 May. (Print after Beechey)**

ABOVE **Major-General Robert Craufurd (1764–1812), commander of the Light Division. A fine light troops leader, the 1810 campaign started badly for Craufurd, who was almost trapped by Marshal Ney's troops at the River Coa, but he was outstanding at Bussaco a few weeks later. He was then sent on leave to England but was back in time to resume command of his division just before the battle of Fuentes de Oñoro.**

TOP **Marshal William Carr Beresford (1768–1854), commander-in-chief of the Portuguese army from 1809 to 1820.**

ABOVE **Major-General Francisco de Silveira (1763–1821) kept the pressure on the French in the northeast with his levies of Portuguese militia and Ordenanza. (Museu Militar do Bussaco)**

ABOVE, RIGHT **Monument to Don Julian Sanchez and his guerrillas in Ciudad Rodrigo. (Photo: RC)**

was concerned with the safety of Porto. He was ably assisted by **Nicholas Trant** and **John Wilson**, two outstanding British officers commanding Portuguese militia brigades south of the Douro River who also wrought havoc on French communications.

This last phase of the campaign in Portugal saw the involvement of some sizeable Spanish forces. **José Caro Marquis de La Romana** led the Spanish corps that joined Wellington at the Lines of Torres Vedras in October 1810. La Romana, who had participated in countless engagements with the French since 1808, always managed to preserve the core of his force in spite of all sorts of hardships. He was not a gifted tactician, but he was nevertheless one of the outstanding generals of the Peninsular War with a cautious and measured character and, contrary to most of his fellow Spanish generals, adopted a spirit of co-operation with Wellington's Anglo-Portuguese army. His sudden death in January 1811 was, as Oman put it, a 'real disaster to the cause of the allies'. A very different type of Spanish leader was the Spanish guerrilla leader **Don Julian Sanchez**. A man of humble circumstances, he waged a 'war to the death' on the French, with personal vengeance high on his agenda as a result of cruelties committed by French troops on his family. From 1811, Sanchez was in regular communication with Wellington, to whom he sent most valuable intelligence. His role in the battle of Fuentes de Oñoro was negligible as this was a contest between regular armies, but his ability to harass the French and to provide outstanding information on the enemy made him valuable to Wellington. Their collaboration continued into Spain and the two were even seen by Sergeant Costello of the 95th Rifles walking together 'linked in arm' in November 1812.

3 Quoted in Michael Barthorp, *Wellington's Generals* (Osprey MAA 84) p.3. Colonel Torrens, the military secretary to the commander-in-chief at the Horse Guards in London, replied with regard to Erskine that 'No doubt he is sometimes a little mad, but in his lucid intervals he is an uncommonly clever fellow'.

OPPOSING ARMIES

General of Division Jean-Gabriel Marchand (1765–1851), He commanded a division in the 6th Corps of Masséna's army.

THE FRENCH

In November 1807, a 25,000-man French army under General Junot had marched into Portugal unopposed, as the population viewed any attempt to resist Napoleon's imperial French army as futile. Less than three years later the situation had changed markedly. The French were no longer seen as invincible and even Marshal Masséna's mighty 'Army of Portugal' had been badly mauled. The army had three corps, each of which had two or three divisions, each division having several brigades. Each French line or light infantry regiment usually had five battalions (four service and one depot), and on paper the regimental establishment totalled 3,908 men including 78 officers. In practice, battalions were much weaker (see Orders of Battle. page 90). The grenadier companies were often grouped into temporary battalions of elite shock troops such as those that attacked the village of Fuentes de Oñoro.

Dragoons formed an important element of Masséna's cavalry and they performed with much bravery at Fuentes de Oñoro. According to a decree of 8 March 1807, a dragoon regiment had four squadrons each of two companies, each company totalling 108 dragoons. On paper, the regiment had 1,044 officers and men with 1,055 horses. The realities of the Portuguese campaign were vastly different, with cavalry companies and squadrons drawn from various regiments to form weak brigades. Monbrun's cavalry reserve, made up of detachments from six dragoon regiments, numbered 1,187 officers and men, barely more than a regiment at establishment strength. The same was true of the hussars and chasseurs à cheval with Masséna's army. Elements of Napoleon's Imperial Guard cavalry joined the army before the battle of Fuentes de

Wellington and his staff, c.1811. He was 'an immortal Mind – Who Pomp repell'd, and Pageantry of Show, And scorn'd the Homage, which from thence did flow; Simply attir'd, he sought th' embattled Plain' according to the author of the humorous *Military Adventures of Johnny Newcome* (London, 1816), who was obviously a veteran of the Peninsula. It was illustrated by T. Rowlandson.

Major-General Sir Stapleton Cotton, later Viscount Cumbermere, commander of Wellington's cavalry. (Print after Pearson)

Brigadier-General Andrew Hay (1762–1814) commanded a brigade consisting of the 3/1st, 1/9th and 2/38th regiments of Foot in the 5th Division from the fall of 1810 and was present at Fuentes de Oñoro although not heavily engaged. (Print after Raeburn)

Oñoro but were not engaged. Of the many deficiencies of Masséna's French army by the end of the campaign, perhaps the most serious was a lack of artillery. This translated into a lack of firepower that was to have a telling effect in the last and most important battle of the campaign, which saw the Allies with a third more guns than the French.

For all its endurance and martial qualities, the French 'Army of Portugal' had a terrible record with regard to what are now termed human rights. There are always such incidents in war but the depredations and inhuman behaviour by many of the officers and soldiers of that army in Portugal were so widespread that they had a decisive effect, not only on the course of the campaign by the French but also on the perception many in Europe had of Napoleon's army. To many, the soldier-champions of 'liberty, equality and fraternity' had become ruthless tyrants.

THE BRITISH

By the autumn of 1810, the British army in Portugal was a well-seasoned force. It amounted to nearly 46,000 men, of which 34,000 were on the effective strength at the Lines of Torres Vedras. The men's morale was high after Bussaco and they were confident they could stop the French and chase them back to the border. This confidence can only have been boosted by the arrival of another 2,300 infantrymen to form the 7th Division. With more artillery and amply supplied, the main weakness of Wellington's British contingent was its lack of cavalry; fewer than 3,000, and these had numerous commitments, so that there were only 1,800 troopers at Fuentes de Oñoro. The army was sub-divided into divisions, brigades and regiments; the latter mostly represented by one battalion of variable strength, each infantry battalion having ten companies including one of elite grenadiers and one of light infantry. The infantry was armed with the dependable India Pattern musket with which it delivered, according to the French, the deadliest volley fire in Europe three times a minute. The infantry tunics were generally red, hence the famous nickname 'redcoats', but the artillery and the light cavalry wore blue, the rifle units dark green. The uniforms were often in tatters after a few months, as many campaign chronicles attest. However, on the whole, the British were much better supplied and paid than their French enemies.

There was no conscription in Britain so the men were, in theory, volunteers although their reasons for enlisting varied greatly. They were, in general, a rough and ready group of individuals with many heavy drinkers. Their generals often found them an unsavoury social group; Picton once said of the 88th – which greatly distinguished itself at Bussaco and Fuentes de Oñoro – that they were 'the blackguards of the army', echoing Wellington's comment that his soldiers were the 'scum of the earth'. It was thought that only by a most severe discipline could they be turned into effective troops. Very few of their infantry or cavalry officers had benefited from a specialised military education, but they had usually received a good general education and were keen students of their profession. Artillery and engineer officers had special professional training and were equal to any comparable corps in Europe.

The British army had a sizeable staff and service corps structure. Wellington and his generals were often frustrated by the bureaucracy of these departments, Wellington's particular 'bête noire' being the Commissariat. This was a branch of the Treasury rather than the War Office, and in fairness was under great strain ensure supplies of food and even money. In 1810–1811, the Commissariat had to provide enormous amounts of rations to the troops behind the Lines of Torres Vedras and also to many civilian refugees but, on the whole, the challenge was met. In the field, Commissariat officials were not always well liked and there was an instance when either General Picton or General Craufurd threatened to hang a commissary officer if he did not bring up the rations to his division. The injured official went for redress to Wellington, who replied: 'did he say that? Then you may depend upon it he will keep his word.'[4]

THE PORTUGUESE

From the time Beresford took over command as marshal in March 1809, the Portuguese army was fundamentally transformed. Massive administrative reforms were brought in to allow it to operate without difficulty alongside the sizeable numbers of British units that were in Portugal. The efficiency of the country's draft system was greatly improved so that the number of regular troops soared. Between a third and half of Wellington's army consisted of Portuguese units, usually integrated within the British divisions. The drill used was now similar to the British army's and command words were taught in English so that, on the battlefield, Portuguese and British units brigaded together would have as few communication problems as possible. Intensive training brought about a proficiency in volley fire and field manoeuvres. The artillery, which had been mainly used for garrison duty, became a large and efficient force in the field alongside the British batteries.

The battle of Bussaco, fought on 27 September 1810, proved that the Portuguese regulars were as steady and dependable as their British comrades. British and French accounts often attribute the sudden improvement in the quality of the Portuguese army to the many British officers that were attached to it. There is no doubt the influence of the 300 or so British officers that served in the Portuguese army during the Peninsular War was a contributory factor to the army's excellence. However, it is also clear, if less often stated, that the replacing of a large number of older, less-inspired gentlemen with more than 2,500 keen, bright young Portuguese officers had a tremendous impact in transforming the force. Britain provided massive numbers of arms and uniforms and paid some 30,000 of the 45,000

Mamelukes of the Imperial Guard, c.1805–12. A detachment of ten officers and 69 troopers was in reserve at Fuentes de Oñoro. (Print after Myrbach)

ABOVE, LEFT **(1st Polish) Lancers and Chasseurs à cheval of the Imperial Guard, 1811. Some 30 officers and 340 troopers of the lancers and 13 officers and 222 troopers of the Chasseurs were in the reserve at Fuentes de Oñoro. (Print after Phillipoteaux)**

ABOVE, RIGHT **Trooper of the Chasseurs à cheval of the Imperial Guard in campaign dress. (Print after Détaille)**

Portuguese regulars. The Portuguese army was not perfect – its cavalry, for example, was weak and ineffective as a shock force. The administrative corps were often deficient and, starved of money from an empty Portuguese treasury, there were often shortages of food and supplies, which the British commissaries occasionally had to supplement as best they could.

The militia and Ordenanza played a very important role during this campaign, acting either as reserve and garrison troops with Wellington's army in the defences of Lisbon or as quasi-guerrilla troops in the north. Nearly all the militia were mobilised and many others formed. Some were well equipped and uniformed, such as the Sobral Ordenanza Artillery, while others often lacked proper arms. Those in the south garrisoned the forts but relatively few of the men saw action. By comparison, the levies in the north of the country were well led by Silveira, Trant and Wilson and considerably hampered the French. Rarely if ever taken into account by British, French and even Portuguese historians are the hundreds of Portuguese officers that led the thousands of irregulars on the northern frontier.[5]

On the whole, Wellington considered the Portuguese component an integral part of his army, expecting it to perform just as well as his British troops if the army was to be effective. On 1 May 1811, writing to Lord Liverpool, he felt 'confident that they [the French] have it not in their power to defeat the [Anglo-Portuguese] Allied army in a general engagement', demonstrating his faith that the Portuguese units could stand their ground with British regiments in battle, which they did for years to come. It was quite an achievement.

THE SPANISH

General La Romana's Spanish troops at the Torres Vedras lines amounted to about 8,000 men. They were drawn from generals La Carrera's and O'Donnell's divisions. The divisions were not complete as some of their units remained in southwest Spain. The Spanish army, having suffered repeated defeats, was in a pitiful state at that time, and Romana's corps probably represented the best of the remaining troops. 'The white Bourbon uniform had entirely disappeared' well over a year earlier so that by 1810, most Spanish infantry wore brown, although blue and grey were not uncommon, or indeed whatever they could get. Wellington was more concerned with the quality of their weapons than uniforms. However, weapons must have been deficient too, as in January 1811, he 'retained 4000 stands of arms and sets of accoutrements … to be delivered to the Spanish troops late under the command of the Marques de la Romana'. Nevertheless, Wellington was pleased to have these reinforcements.[6]

As the Anglo-Portuguese army approached the Spanish border in the spring of 1811, it came into contact with the guerrilla bands of Don Julian Sanchez, Oliveria and El Frayle which operated in the areas of Ciudad Rodrigo and Salamanca. Their numbers were estimated at about 700, with the most important being Don Juan Sanchez's band of about 500 lancers on the plains of Leon. He joined the Allied army at Fuentes de Oñoro on 3 May 1811 with an unknown number of his men, but these irregulars could be of little assistance when the French cavalry moved against the Allied's southern flank two days later.

Officer of the 12th Chasseur à cheval in summer dress. Many Chasseurs officers had white hussar-style uniforms made of lightweight material in the Peninsula to wear on informal occasions. (Print after M. Orange)

4 As quoted in Arthur Griffiths, *The Wellington Memorial* (London, 1897), p.235. There were good reasons for some suspicions of commissaries and paymasters on the part of the serving officers. They seemed to prosper rather well adding weight to the notion that the office of paymaster could provide 'ample opportunity for self-enrichment' – John Stuart Omond, *Parliament and the Army* (Cambridge, 1933) p.117. The Commissariat was not always a sterling example of administrative excellence. Suffice it to say here that the Deputy Assistant Commissary-General in the Peninsula was court-martialled and dismissed for fiscal embezzlement in 1812.

5 A rich field of study would consider not only the fighting these troops did – still a largely unexplored subject – but also the logistics, command and control with which they operated. Their discipline must have been fairly good as, in general, the wanton killings and inhumane savagery commonly directed at French prisoners by the Spanish guerrillas was relatively rare in Portugal.

6 Lieutenant-Colonel. Gurwood, ed., *The Dispatches of Field Marshal the Duke of Wellington* (London, 1838), VII, 204.

THE LINES OF TORRES VEDRAS

The original Portuguese plan

The idea of the Lines of Torres Vedras is generally thought to have been developed by Lord Wellington in late 1809, with the design carried out by British Royal Engineers officers Richard Fletcher and John Jones. The achievements of these men in the construction of these works are undeniable; their work was tireless and carried out with great talent. In their reports, the British officers understandably emphasised their own role in the general supervision of the construction of the lines. This was natural given the command structure as Fletcher and Jones had the overall responsibility for the supervision of the construction of the lines and reported to Wellington. The reports and the memoirs of these and other officers were eventually published in Britain after the Peninsular War. As a result, the English-speaking public were led to believe that, apart from the thousands of Portuguese peasants who provided the manual labour to build the various works and a few Portuguese military engineers, the entire system had been conceived and the construction directed by British military engineers.

In fact, the idea of building a line of defence between the Atlantic Ocean and the Tagus River had been considered by Portuguese military planners since the latter part of the 18th century. However, at the time there was no threat to Lisbon and such schemes remained entirely theoretical. The British took a similar approach and their first plan was conceived in 1799 by General Sir Charles Stuart, who commanded the British and Émigré troops posted in Portugal. In 1802, the Portuguese government resolved that a topographical map of the country should be made and Lieutenant-Colonel Carlos Frederico Bernardo de Caula was put in charge of the work. He was helped by Captain José Maria das Neves Costa. These engineer officers naturally saw the possibilities for a line of defence north of Lisbon. As a result the initial plans for such fortifications were drawn up by Captain Neves Costa in 1806 and 1807. Indeed, it was Colonel Charles Vincent of the French Imperial Corps of Engineers who next saw the possibilities. He was with General Junot's army that invaded and occupied Portugal in November and December 1807, learned of Caula's and Neves Costa's work and submitted a proposal to Junot in early 1808 for building fortifications north of Lisbon. Nothing was done, although Napoleon later felt that Junot and his army would have been saved by such works. From October 1808, after the French had been compelled to evacuate Portugal, Neves Costa was appointed to draw up a detailed plan. It was a huge project. Neves Costa finished the plans on 4 March 1809 and the accompanying memorandum on 6 June. They were then presented to Wellington for consideration. From that point the plan became a British responsibility.

A peasant of Torres Vedras, c. 1810. Thousands of such men were drafted to build the works forming the lines. Print after Bradford. (Pedro de Brito Collection, Porto)

ABOVE **Colonel Shée of the 13th Chasseurs à cheval, c.1812. There were 20 officers and 250 troopers of the 13th engaged at Fuentes de Oñoro.**

RIGHT **The Lines of Torres Vedras and the fortifications near Lisbon, 1810–11. The 3rd and 2nd lines had mostly British troops and are shown in red whereas the 1st line had mixed Portuguese (yellow) and British (red) garrisons. The French are shown in green. The positions towards the top of the map are those during the French retreat in the spring of 1811. (Luz Soriano, III)**

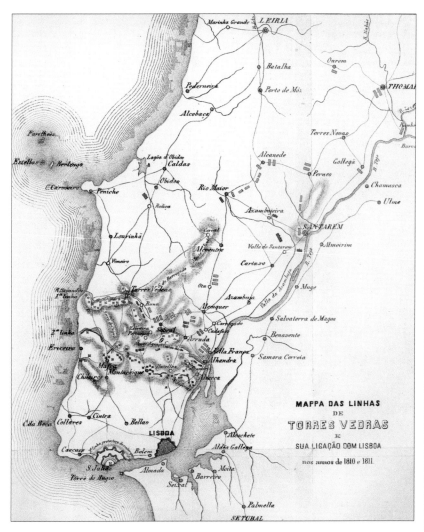

Wellington had his own engineers with his British army in Portugal, and he called on them to evaluate Neves Costa's plan. The idea of a defence line north of Lisbon had interested him when in Portugal in August and September 1808. He had then seen the late General Stuart's plan made nine years before, as well as Colonel Vincent's proposal. Now, with Neves Costa's detailed work, the notion could be put to the test. In October 1809, Wellington took the time to survey the area for himself guided by Neves Costa's maps and accompanied by his senior engineer, Lieutenant-Colonel Richard Fletcher and the quartermaster-generals of the British and Portuguese armies. The reconnaissance was thorough and when it was over, Wellington had seen just about every hill, valley, river and road between the Atlantic and the Tagus north of Lisbon.

Lines Ordered Built by Wellington

To his everlasting credit, Wellington made the decision to go ahead and build the proposed defences. On 20 October 1809, Wellington sent Lieutenant-Colonel Fletcher a long and detailed instruction regarding the works to be prepared. There would be two lines of redoubts and trenches on two ranges of hills. The first and most northerly, running

Maréchal-des-logis (Sergeant) Le Saché, 22nd Chasseurs à cheval, 1810. Apart from wearing a shako instead of a bicorn, the dress shown was much the same during the campaign. The 22nd was part of Reynier's 2nd Corps.

from the estuary of the Zizandre River on the Atlantic through Torres Vedras to Alhandra on the west bank of the Tagus, would have four large redoubts capable of holding several thousand men each at the towns of Torres Vedras, Sobral, Arruda and Alhandra. A second line would be built between Carvoeira and Alverca should the French break through the first line. Naturally, there were changes made by Wellington's British engineers, in particular that a large defensive position be built at the entrance of the Tagus River. This was the last line of defence in case the lines could not be held and the army should have to be evacuated by sea. Neves Costa's plan had called instead for an all-out defence of Lisbon.

There were various other adjustments, but on the whole Neves Costa's plan of a line of fortified positions remained the basis of the defences.[7]

Captain Jones, who later became the British 'historian of the Lines', attributed the supervision of the construction to Lieutenant-Colonel Fletcher and himself along with three Royal Engineers captains, eight lieutenants, a captain and a lieutenant of the King's German Legion engineers and, lastly, to three lieutenants of the Portuguese engineers. Besides these officers named by Jones, at least six more British engineer officers worked on the lines. Some 20 British engineer officers thus worked at erecting 154 fortified works, some of them quite extensive, which made up the lines as well as repairing existing forts and building other works on the coast.[8]

As the Portuguese Royal Corps of Engineers had over 90 officers in the country, one might wonder as to why so few Portuguese engineers worked on the lines. The answer, as furnished by the service records of Portuguese engineer officers, is that at least 39 of them did in fact work on the construction of the lines and other related fortifications in the Lisbon area. This makes much more sense and explains where many of the Portuguese officers were and what they were doing.[9]

The three Portuguese engineers mentioned by Captain Jones worked under the direct supervision of the British Royal Engineers. At first glance, this could be the reason why only they were given credit for the work. Jones would naturally report on the work of his own British Royal Engineers. But again the service records indicate that there were nine rather than three officers of the Portuguese Royal Corps of Engineers who were detached serving 'under the orders of Lt. Col. Fletcher'. Another two were reported under Captain 'Squier' (Squire) of the British Royal Engineers in January 1811. All this data indicates that the numbers of British, and especially of Portuguese, engineers working on the fortifications were substantially higher. There were therefore some 20 British and nine Portuguese engineers working under Fletcher's direct orders and about 30 other Portuguese engineers working elsewhere on the line or in related works being erected in 1809–10.[10]

The scenery in the area of the Lines of Torres Vedras between Cadafaes and Arruda that largely escaped development. Then as now, small windmills were a common sight on the hills. (Photo: RC)

ABOVE, LEFT **French 27th Light Infantry and 5th Chasseurs à cheval, c.1811–12. The 27th is shown with white waistcoat and trousers, more suitable in the Peninsula's heat than the regulation blue. The Chasseur à cheval wears the fur busby indicating he is an elite trooper. (Print after Goddard and Booth)**

ABOVE, RIGHT **Grenadier officer of the French 94th Line Infantry, c.1811–12. A battalion of this regiment was in the 9th Corps at Fuentes de Oñoro. (Print after Goddard and Booth)**

What all these engineers were asked to build was a most innovative work. The 'lines' were not a continuous wall such as Hadrian's Wall or the Wall of China. The works that had been conceived by the Allied engineers and reviewed by Wellington, were a complex and numerous set of redoubts, forts and trenches, the first example in modern history of defences in depth on such a vast scale. Great numbers of fortifications would be built on top of hills strung out in the two lines. The fields of fire of these forts would be largely overlapping so that an attack on any fort would always be caught in the crossfire from those on either side. In addition, innumerable trenches and other obstacles further linked and strengthened the system.

The heights of Almada overlooked the River Tagus and the city of Lisbon from the south. It was possible that a strong French force could outflank the lines by marching down on the east bank of the Tagus and occupy the heights. Should this occur, the French would then be able to block the Tagus and bombard Lisbon. The older forts at Almada were therefore refurbished and 17 new redoubts spread over 7 km built inland. These works were equipped with 86 guns and could accommodate up to 7,500 men. A telegraph station was installed to communicate with the lines. Detachments of militia and the Lisbon Royal Commerce Volunteers manned these works.

The final work built east of Lisbon was a semi-circular line of defences at Sao Juliao (or St. Julian). It was called the 3rd Line. Should the lines above Lisbon collapse under the French army's attacks, the British and Portuguese troops that could, were to fall back to this point to embark on vessels that would evacuate the army. A strong fort was built outside this fortified enclosure and within it were redoubts and four large jetties to embark the troops. Wellington may not have believed he would ever have to evacuate the Allied army, but it was a safe measure to take which also reassured the politicians.

On 6 October Wellington divided the two lines above Lisbon into six districts and assigned garrisons for their forts. Almada and Sao Juliao were not included in this system as they constituted a last redoubt. Neither was the flotilla on the Tagus nor the troops detached east of the Tagus who were mostly watching for French movements in the general area of Santarem. Finally, there was the fortress of Peniche at the end of a narrow peninsula on the Atlantic situated north of Masséna's army. Peniche was the general training centre for the Portuguese infantry, and it was unlikely that Masséna would commit a substantial part of his army to take it, as this would further weaken his force at the Lines of Torres Vedras. He did not attempt to take Peniche but remained worried that the British might use it to land troops and attack his rear. A cordon of French troops stood guard outside the Peniche peninsula to warn Masséna of any such movement.

The Lines of Torres Vedras – Administrative Districts

District No. 1. From Torres Vedras to the sea.
HQ Torres Vedras.
2,470 militia infantry, 250 Ordenanza artillery, 140 regular Portuguese artillery, 70 British artillery.

District No. 2. From Sobral de Monte Agraço to the valley of Calhandriz.
HQ Sobral de Monte Agraço.
1,300 militia infantry, 300 Ordenanza artillery, 140 regular Portuguese artillery, 40 British artillery.

District No. 3. From Alhandra to the valley of Calhandriz.
HQ Alhandra.
400 militia infantry, 60 Ordenanza artillery, 60 British artillery.

District No. 4. From the banks of the Tagus to the valley of Calhandriz.
HQ Bucellas.
1,100 militia infantry, 500 Ordenanza artillery, 80 regular Portuguese artillery.

District No. 5. From the pass of Freixal to the right of the pass of Mafra.
HQ Montachique.
2,400 militia infantry, 480 Ordenanza artillery, 120 regular Portuguese artillery, 50 British artillery.

District No. 6. From the pass of Mafra to the sea.
HQ Mafra.
700 militia infantry, 350 Ordenanza artillery, 230 regular Portuguese artillery, 40 British artillery.

Officer of the Royal Engineers, c.1802. Until 1813, the engineers had a blue uniform faced with black velvet and gold buttons. C.C.P. Lawson after Loftie. (Anne S.K. Brown Military Collection, Brown University, Providence, USA)

Evacuation of the countryside

The forbearance of the Portuguese people through this most tragic period in their country's history was extraordinary and admirable. When the French invaders crossed into Portugal hundreds of thousands of civilians fled before them and found refuge behind the Lines of Torres Vedras; their last hope. Sir John Colborne of the 52nd Light Infantry wrote to his sister of the distress he witnessed in the town of Alhandra, where the 'unfortunate inhabitants' had 'all left their houses, and their furniture, poor people, is converted into barriers, &c. How should you like to see your piano, your writing tables, chairs and trunks heaped together at the south end of Sloane street to impede the enemy's march?' he painfully asked. But the tragedy was, in fact, striking a large part of the population and Colborne, no doubt like all who witnessed it, was profoundly affected. He confided that he had 'never seen so much distress and misery experienced by the mass of the people as in the late flight of the inhabitants towards the capital. Not a person remained in his home, whole towns and villages decamped, taking with them only what a cart could convey, and leaving the rest of their property to be pillaged by the armies of friends and enemies.'[11]

Captain John Jones of the Royal Engineers saw the 'immense crowds of fugitive Portuguese – men, women and children' come into the Lines of Torres Vedras, blocking every road. As if the sorrow of their flight from the French was not enough, the 'autumnal rains set in at this very moment, pouring down in torrents, accompanied by severe thunder and lightning, filling the streams and watercourses, and rendering the roads deep and heavy'. Such conditions added to the utter misery of a desperate situation that countless innocents had been plunged into.

Tens of thousands of refugees who abandoned their homes as the French army approached found safety behind the Lines of Torres Vedras in the autumn of 1810. Most were ruined by the invasion, their livelihood and homes destroyed and their hardships such that many once prosperous families were reduced to begging for food. This contemporary print shows a great crowd of refugees at a food distribution point at the convent of Arroios in Lisbon. (Museu Militar do Bussaco)

7 Wellington never actually saw Neves Costa but nevertheless in 1812 criticised his work as being inaccurate and needing to be redone. However, the lines as built largely followed Neves Costa's suggestions. The background on the various plans of the lines and on the work of Neves Costa is given in Maghaleas Sepulveda, *Historia Organica* …, XIII.

8 The British officers mentioned by Jones were Captains William C. Holloway, J. Williams, S. Dickinson and Wedekind (KGL), Lieutenants F. Stanway, A. Thomson, W. Forster, S. Trench, R.S. Piper, H.A. Tapp, William Reid, J.L. Hulme and Meinecke (KGL). The three Portuguese officers are named as Lieutenants Lourenzo Homem, Souza and Britto. They were actually Majors Lourenço Homem da Cunha de Eça, Manuel Joaquim Brandao de Sousa and Captain Joaquim Norberto Xavier de Brito. The other British officers were Captains George Ross, S.R. Chapman, J. Squire and Henry Goldfinch, E. Mulcaster, P. Wright and Rice-Jones. Captain John Burgoyne and Lieutenant Stanway were also at the lines, along with the engineers with Wellington's Allied army, which retired behind the line in early October 1810. These did not participate in the building but were used to supervise upkeep. From 6 October, engineers were assigned to each district as follows: No. 1: Captain Mulcaster and Lieutenant Thompson, No. 2: Captain Goldfinch and Lieutenant Forster, No. 3: Captain Squire and Lieutenant Piper, No. 4: Captain Burgoyne and Lieutenant Stanway, No. 5: Captain Dickenson and Lieutenant Trench, No. 6: Captain Ross and Lieutenant Hulme. W. Porter, History of the Corps of Royal Engineers (London, 1889), Vol. 1, has 20 Royal Engineer officers working on the lines. There were also 18 Royal Sappers and Miners supervising labourers.

9 In 1812, Halliday reported that the Portuguese Royal Corps of Engineers consisted of eight colonels, 13 lieutenant-colonels, 27 majors, 22 captains, 11 first lieutenants and 11 second lieutenants for a total of 92 officers. This is confirmed in Maghaleas Sepulveda, *Historia Organica*…, V, which is a detailed history of the Portuguese engineers to 1816. The service records of Portuguese officers are on pp. 308–320 of which 39 are reported as having worked on the lines. The services of 36 others show them on every front, many serving with the Allied army until 1814.

10 The six other Portuguese officers were: Francisco Antonio Raposo, Bernardo José Pereira dos Santos Franco, Francisco Villela Barboza, Luis Maximo Jorge de Bellegarde, Joao Antonio d'Almeida Cibrao and Henrique Luiz Aschoff. Joaquim Pedro Pinto de Sousa and Jacvinto Joaquim Torcato Xavier were under Squire in January 1811. See Maghaleas Sepulveda, *Historia Organica*…, V for details. This somewhat contradicts most British accounts and histories published since the 19th century but Portuguese sources have, unfortunately, usually been ignored in most English-language publications. Sir Charles Oman did use them, notably Luz Soriano's *Historia da Guerra Civil*, but his volumes appeared before Maghaleas Sepulveda's detailed studies in the 1910s and 20s. Prof. David Horward has also made extensive use of Portuguese sources.

11 Sir John Colborne to his sister Alethea, Alhandra, 9 November 1810, in Moore Smith, *The Life of John Colborne*, p.146.

THE FRENCH FACE THE LINES

According to Marbot who was on Masséna's staff, when the French senior officers first saw the lines there was a damaging impact upon the army's morale. They bitterly criticised Masséna's decision to attack the Anglo-Portuguese at Bussaco two weeks earlier instead of simply trying to turn Wellington's position, which he had successfully achieved after that battle. The battle of Bussaco had resulted in very high casualties to the French army and had shaken its morale. Until then it was intact and in high spirits in spite of the difficulties of the terrain. Had Masséna not wasted the army at Bussaco, many believed the Lines of Torres Vedras could have been attacked as soon as they were reached by men full of ardour and confidence. Few Frenchmen doubted that, in such conditions, they would have reached Sintra with little

Gunners of the Royal Artillery, 1807. Apart from pantaloons in the field, the dress of the gunners was essentially the same in 1810–11. Print after Atkinson. (Anne S.K. Brown Military Collection, Brown University, Providence, USA)

OVERLEAF
This scene is typical of the dozens of forts along the Lines of Torres Vedras. Some of the strongest works were south of the village of Sobral, which the French probed without success in mid-October. There was a large redoubt on Mount Agraço but the area was defended by a total of seven forts with 55 guns and a garrison of 3,000 men. Most of the gunners were from the Sobral Ordenanza Artillery shown here. One of their officers looks on accompanied by an officer of the British Royal Engineers in his blue faced black uniform. The guns shown are Portuguese Gribeauval-style pieces mounted on British-type single block carriages. (Patrice Courcelle)

difficulty. However, the effects of Bussaco had undermined the confidence of senior officers and their ADCs as to the ability of the army to assault these new fortifications. There was much dispute and disagreement about the strength of the lines; small hills with minor forts were now seen as 'new mountains of Bussaco whose capture would cost torrents of blood', Masséna was told by his officers.

The marshal was determined to have some sort of demonstration. To not assault the lines, or at the very least to probe them, was unthinkable if not in the minds of his staff officers, then certainly in that of his imperial master. It was as much a matter of military honour as of strategy – some sort of attempt had to be made. To do nothing would be the epitome of 'lâcheté' – unforgivable slovenliness that would be unpardonable, not only for the emperor but for French public opinion and especially the rest of the army.

THE PROBES AT SOBRAL

Faced with the necessity to do something, the heated disagreements amongst his staff and the extensive and foreboding line of fortifications along his southern skyline, Masséna was in a dilemma. Of the senior corps commanders, General Junot favoured an all-out assault on a weaker point in the lines. He knew Lisbon and its area from his time

Soldiers of the Foot Guards, 1807. Apart from the disappearance of queues and powdered hair in 1808, the appearance of the Foot Guards brigade in Wellington's army would have been close to that shown in this print. Bearskin caps were not worn in the Peninsula but white linen pantaloons were. Print after Atkinson. (Anne S.K. Brown Military Collection, Brown University, Providence, USA)

there in 1807–08 and felt it was impossible to defend such a huge area in depth. Once a breach was made, he reasoned that Wellington would be unable to contain it as his reserves would be too scattered to mount an effective counter-attack. In his view, once through the lines a push could be made on Sintra and then on Lisbon.

Marshal Ney and General Reynier both disagreed and argued vehemently that the reconnaissances made so far indicated the Anglo-Portuguese positions were powerful and that Wellington would doubtless have more surprises behind the Torres Vedras–Alhandra line. They pointed to the many such surprises the French had encountered at Bussaco, which had cost them so dear. The French do not seem to have fully appreciated at this time that a second powerful line existed; nor that there were entrenchments built around the limits of Lisbon and that the Fort Sao Juliao area had been transformed into a vast fortified camp as a possible last redoubt. In hindsight, it would seem that Ney and Reynier were right to urge caution.

It was agreed, nevertheless, that some sort of probe should be attempted. Junot's 8th Corps, which had been held in reserve at Bussaco was selected for the task. It was deployed in the area north of Sobral. Of the various works and villages forming the line, the abandoned hamlet of Sobral seemed the most promising for an attack as it had no defences other than insubstantial barricades for the troops inside it and a few weak positions on the hills just behind. There seemed to be other stronger works further south, but these were too deep within the line to be properly assessed by the French scouts.

Here was one of the Anglo-Portuguese army's first surprises for Masséna and his men. The village of Sobral was in fact a false position. Wellington had extended his skirmish line on a rough arc with Sobral as its focus but, in truth, the real first line was at Mount Agraço about a kilometre southeast of the village. Here a formidable redoubt had been built, festooned with artillery and served by a strong garrison. Amongst these soldiers were some 331 officers and men of the Sobral Ordenanza Artillery who had particular scores to settle with the French whom they knew would ruin what remained of their native village. These villagers trained hard to master the fine art of gunnery, were proud of their splendid uniforms of local brown cloth, trimmed with black and scarlet, and they were ready to fight alongside their regular comrades of the Portuguese and British artillery. Wellington's HQ was at Pero Negro, a short ride to the southwest, so that the men posted in the Great Redoubt were graced by a visit and the encouragement of their commander-in-chief every morning. Unsurprisingly, the morale of the defenders of the Sobral area could not have been higher.

By contrast Masséna was nowhere to be seen amongst his troops opposite the lines. He remained in the rear at his HQ in Alemquer, doubtless detained by the charms of his mistress, Madame X. At the front General Montbrun identified the lines of fortifications on 11 October and many of the senior officers surveyed them the following day. It was in the afternoon of that day, 12 October, that the French army suffered a tragic loss. Brigadier General Sainte-Croix was a brilliant cavalry officer and one of the army's best commanders who also had a positive influence on Masséna. He was with a party of his cavalrymen surveying the eastern end of the lines along the Tagus River when a British

Private of the 2nd Foot, c.1808–11. A good view of the appearance of British troops on campaign. (Anne S.K. Brown Military Collection, Brown University, Providence, USA)

gunboat, seeing movement on the banks of the river, opened fire on what were obviously French troopers. A moment later Sainte-Croix was cut in two by a cannon ball. This 'lucky shot' was a grievous loss of a popular officer and was noted in many French accounts. In addition Masséna had lost one of his best advisors, a man who combined acute tactical skills with daring. Nevertheless, Masséna remained in the rear while instructing the 8th Corps to move up.

General Junot had no way of knowing that his 8th Corps' 12,000 men were hopelessly out-numbered. However, he prudently advanced his corps on a wide front towards Sobral. During the afternoon of 12 October the advance parties of French troops under Brigadier-General Bertrand Clausel reached the village of Sobral, and a fusillade broke out between the men of General Clausel's Division and skirmishers from the 71st Highland Light Infantry, the King's German Legion and the 5th (Rifle) battalion of the 60th Foot. The British troops were driven out of the village by masses of French infantrymen but continued to skirmish with the French from the hills behind Sobral.

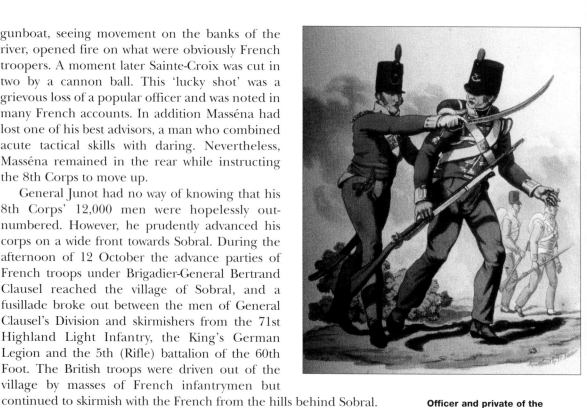

Officer and private of the 52nd Light Infantry, which was part of the Light Division. Print after C.H. Smith. (Anne S.K. Brown Military Collection, Brown University, Providence, USA)

On the British side, Wellington's scouts reported movements in the French army during the night of 12–13 October that convinced him that the most likely target would be Sobral. Accordingly, he ordered the four divisions of generals Cole, Picton, Campbell and Spencer to that area and Pack's Portuguese brigade to join the garrison already inside the Sobral redoubt. La Romana's Spanish corps was also nearby. Within a few hours, over 30,000 men were deployed along a 7-km front ready to meet an attack south of Sobral.

On 13 October, Clausel's Division moved south and soon encountered skirmishers and light infantry pickets of the 7th Foot and the Brunswick-Oels Corps from Cole's Division. Outnumbered, Cole's men retreated until he sent the light companies of the 11th and 23rd Portuguese Infantry from Harvey's Brigade. Junot sent Gratien's Brigade to reinforce his voltigeurs and a fierce fight ensued which lasted several hours until Harvey's men withdrew closer to Mount Agraço and its redoubt. Harvey, 'a very excellent officer' in D'Urban's opinion, was wounded in the affair.

Early the next morning, Junot renewed the attack with the help of some field artillery to drive out the picket line of the 71st (Highland Light Infantry), which had erected some barricades. French infantry then drove out the skirmishers of the 71st but the Highland light infantrymen now regrouped and counter-attacked, driving the surprised French back all the way to the houses on the edge of the village of Sobral. There they were halted by Clausel's Division and the 71st returned to its position unmolested. The situation was a stand-off.

In the meantime Masséna had at last arrived at the front, witnessed the skirmish and finally saw the lines for himself. He climbed a hill with his staff officers south of Sobral and, next to a windmill, dismounted to examine the terrain. A shot from a cannon on Mount Agraço warned him that he was getting too close and he is said to have acknowledged the shot and ridden away. Pellet noted Masséna's disappointment at seeing steep hills covered in fortifications rather than the 'undulating accessible plateau' he expected. He was especially upset with the renegade Portuguese officers for failing to inform him fully about the mountains north of Lisbon. They replied that they could not know about the works recently built by the Anglo-Portuguese, to which he snapped that the unexpected mountains had not been built by Wellington! There was not much that could be done. Junot called off the probe by

Officer and private of the Light Company, 85th Foot, 1809–11. On campaign, pantaloons were usually worn. (Print after P.W. Reynolds)

Clausel's Division and Masséna did not order a new attack. The British and Portuguese suffered 67 casualties, the French about 150.

The skirmish around Sobral had momentous consequences as it convinced Masséna that it was impossible to smash the lines with the forces at his disposal. He now knew that there were two other lines behind the first one he had seen. The forces under Wellington's command seemed very strong while his own were diminishing. Masséna estimated that Wellington had 60,000 British and Portuguese regular troops plus another 50,000 'armed peasants' and militia manning the Lines of Torres Vedras, while he himself now had only about 50,000 French army regulars. Wellington in fact had about 77,000 men including the Spanish corps.

As October drew to a close, Masséna found himself almost isolated. His conquest of Portugal could potentially turn into a disaster. To his front was an imposing network of field fortifications; his rear swarmed with hostile irregular troops, who were a constant hindrance and impossible to eliminate. He had crossed into Portugal with about 65,000 men in the summer of 1810 and he now had about 15,000 less. He needed more men; no additional large-scale attacks could be mounted without reinforcements and he wrote asking that at least another corps should join his army.

In the Anglo-Portuguese camp, Wellington was very optimistic at the turn of events. As early as 27 October, a month to the day after the battle of Bussaco and little more than two weeks after he had withdrawn his army into the Lines of Torres Vedras, Wellington was writing to his brother William Wellesley-Pole from his headquarters at Pero Negro that 'all is going well as possible … I think the French must retire; & I don't

These British 'Soldiers on a March' are shown with their women and children, 'who followed the drum' as camp followers, an often forgotten reality of Wellington's army. Print by Rowlandson published on 1 April 1811. (Anne S.K. Brown Military Collection, Brown University, Providence, USA)

ABOVE **German soldiers of the Brunswick-Oels Corps, c.1811–12. Wellington's army included German units, gathering men mostly from Hanover and Brunswick. Elements of the Brunswick-Oels Corps, a light infantry and rifles unit, were spread in the 4th, 5th and 7th divisions. From left to right, a rifleman, a light infantryman and a hussar. (Print after Goddard and Booth)**

RIGHT **A private of the Lisbon Police Guard and an 'armed peasant' of the Algarve Ordenanza, c.1809–11. Print after Bradford. (Pedro de Brito Collection, Porto)**

know of any reinforcement they can get for their Army of which I need entertain any apprehension.'[12]

Retaking the countryside

While Masséna's army was encamped before the lines, Portuguese troops made up largely of militia and Ordenanza regained control of much of the devastated countryside to the north. Leiria had been reoccupied by General John Wilson's Portuguese militias while Colonel Nicholas Trant's levies continued to hold Coimbra and points south. Other levies were at Castelo Branco to the southeast. While this was not a direct threat, as such troops could never match regulars, the French army nevertheless had to be mindful of events in its rear areas. Stragglers and small parties were sure to run into trouble if they ventured too far.

Much further to the northeast, General Francisco Silveira had come down from the Douro with his Portuguese levies towards the northeastern border with Spain. Silveira's men were mostly embodied militiamen and Ordenanza from Tras os Montes with regulars of the 24th Line Infantry Regiment. Their numbers were uncertain and surely varied greatly. They could not resist a direct attack by a strong French force but they were led by a general who was outstanding in his leadership of irregulars (see Campaign 90 *Vimeiro 1808*). His troops reached the vicinity of the fortress of Almeida towards the end of October and surrounded it. The Portuguese drove in the French 'Foragers and Outposts, compelled the Garrison to shut the Gates and in fact placed it in a state of siege.'[13] No supplies could enter the town. This was not a formal siege as there could be no bombardment and strong French parties might come out but they could not venture too far from the fortress or they would be overwhelmed. The French in Almeida found themselves surrounded and cut off to the west by Silveira's men and by the Spanish guerrillas of Don Julian Sanchez to the east towards Ciudad Rodrigo. Although the Portuguese and the Spanish never had a warm opinion of each other, old rivalries were largely put aside during the Peninsular War and they joined forces against the common foe. It is evident that, on the northeast border, General Silveira and Don Julian Sanchez were in close collaboration. As a result, Masséna's communications with the French armies in Spain and with France became next to impossible as couriers were almost sure to be intercepted.

The Portuguese countryside that Masséna's French army had crossed was devastated and abandoned so that food and forage were very hard to find near the lines. The occupied part of Portugal was entirely deserted by the Portuguese. There was no way the French authorities could manage the resources it might still contain as its vanished inhabitants were simply not there to obey orders from the French commissariat. In other occupied countries, after an initial shock and some painful incidents, a sort of live-and-let-live arrangement eventually came about as local merchants would sell foodstuffs and supplies to the French armies, and its soldiers would eventually fraternise with the local population. A puppet government of sorts would be put in place and life would go on.

In Portugal, from the outset with the first occupation by General Junot in November 1808, the greed and cruelty of generals such as Loison had led to indiscriminate looting, and the torture and death of countless Portuguese. In spite of barbaric and near-genocidal practices by the French soldiers in such places as Coimbra, the cycle of cruelty went on. Finding no supplies, each French regiment at the Lines of Torres Vedras formed detachments to roam the back country in search of anything edible, and as Marshal Marmont later recalled, if a Portuguese was so unfortunate as to fall into their hands, they would 'put him under torture so as to obtain indications and revelations as to where

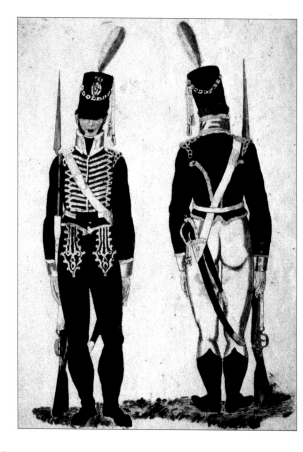

Front and back view of an infantryman of the Lisbon Royal Commerce Volunteers in full dress, c. 1810. Composed of merchants and gentlemen of Lisbon 'magnificently appointed at their own expense' in brown uniforms, the unit, which consisted of some 1,300 hussars and infantry who performed garrison duties 'in the town with the greatest zeal and regularity' according to William Warre. (Pedro de Brito Collection, Porto)

were the foodstuffs hidden.' The soldiers would hang the unfortunate person initially 'au rouge' (meaning over a fire to roast him) as a threat to other Portuguese then 'au bleu' (seemingly prods with edged weapons or beaten black and blue with sticks and musket butts) until 'death arrived'.

Naturally, the French parties performing such deeds did not always get away, quite literally, with murder. Every day 'isolated men were massacred by peasants' of the Ordenanza and 'entire detachments' would vanish so that the French 'losses became immense' on the fringes of the army. However, Marmont recalled, the worst menace to the existence of Masséna's army at the Lines of Torres Vedras was that 'all discipline having disappeared, it presented at the highest degree a spectacle of confusion and of disorder.'[14]

General Foy's Mission

Masséna needed reinforcements and advice from Napoleon. General Maximilien Foy was entrusted with taking dispatches from Masséna all the way to the emperor in Paris and was escorted by the 4th Battalion of the 47th Line Regiment and 120 cavalry, in all some 500 men. Foy left at the end of October and reached Ciudad Rodrigo on 8 November. From there he did not need such a strong escort, and most of the men were left behind while he went on to France, reaching Paris on 21 November.

The emperor received him with Masséna's dispatches the following day. Napoleon wished to know more and invited Foy into his study. For the next two hours, Napoleon submitted Foy to a gruelling session of questions and comments. He deplored Masséna's decision to attack Wellington at Bussaco, blamed him for the loss of Coimbra and lauded the courage and determination of the British. He felt that Masséna and Ney had underestimated the British, although Reynier knew better having been beaten twice by them (in Egypt and at Maida in Italy). Having failed to drive the British out of Portugal, Napoleon reflected that the course to follow was to wear them down as he had far more troops than they did and could keep up the struggle for longer.

Napoleon had numerous opinions as to what to do next. Masséna 'must take Abrantes – Elvas would be no good to us' and his army must remain in front of the lines north of Lisbon otherwise a disaster was feared. Assistance and reinforcements were certainly needed and Napoleon said that Marshal Edouard Mortier's 5th Corps would be ordered to move into Portugal, wondering at the same time if the order would be carried out. Even before Foy had arrived in Paris, Napoleon had guessed that Masséna needed help and sent orders to General Jean-Baptiste Drouet d'Erlon's 9th Corps to march to Almeida and open up the line of communication with Masséna. Marshal Nicolas Soult in southern Spain was also told to move towards Portugal

Napoleon saw Foy again on 24 November but nothing really decisive was done. The emperor seemed strangely powerless when faced with the problems in Portugal and Spain. He mused it was a great distance away for his orders to be carried out and seemed content to leave the place to his bickering generals and marshals, with no clear commander-in-chief for the French armies in the Peninsula.

MASSÉNA'S CHOICES

With his army before the lines, Masséna had four broad strategic choices as to what to do next with his Army of Portugal. Firstly he could attack the Lines of Torres Vedras; secondly he could return to the Portuguese/Spanish border and hold Almeida and Ciudad Rodrigo. A third option was to march north, take Porto and hold the northern bank of the Douro River. Finally, he could cross the Tagus River to its east bank, march into Alentejo province and occupy the heights of Almada at the entrance of the Tagus opposite Lisbon.

The first choice, to attack the lines, was clearly folly and he had no intention of committing his men to that task. A return to the border of Portugal and Spain meant the end of the campaign and, to a certain extent, the defeat of the French invasion of Portugal. However, it also

Peasant infantry of the Ciudad Rodrigo area 'militia' c. 1810–11; no doubt one of the patriot guerrillas led by Don Julian Sanchez. Print after Bradford. (Pedro de Brito Collection, Porto)

meant that the French army would remain relatively intact and could be reinforced for another try later on. The Anglo-Portuguese would remain under a powerful threat of invasion and would have to remain on the defensive; this was the option favoured by Marshal Ney. The third choice – take Porto and hold the northern bank of the Douro – would keep the French army on the offensive in Portugal by seizing the country's second most important city and harnessing its many resources. The French army could rest and recuperate while secure on the northern bank of the Douro. But this course would have little decisive effect, as to conquer Portugal one must take Lisbon.

The final choice, to cross the Tagus River and occupy its east bank, made much sense, as this would have given the famished army fresh areas from which to draw food and supplies, having exhausted the country north of Lisbon. The heights of Almada would have fallen and French batteries would then command much of the naval traffic to Lisbon. The rear of the French army would have contained almost no Allied troops except for the garrison of Elvas on the Spanish border. Part of the French army in southern Spain could have blockaded Elvas and linked with the Army of Portugal.

This last choice also retained the initiative with the French army which, if supplied and reinforced, would be in place to try to beat the Allied army and take Lisbon at the first opportunity. In his memoirs, Marshal Marmont, who later succeeded Masséna in the command of the Army of Portugal, stated he favoured the fourth option and, as Foy mentioned, so did Napoleon.

This hill just south of Sobral had fortifications on its top in 1810. The site is now occupied by various city works but a military appearance has been retained. (Photo: RC)

Retreat to Santarem

But even as the emperor was saying that the army must remain before Lisbon, Masséna was seriously thinking of retiring from the lines where he could accomplish little and where his army was nearly starving. Yet he also wanted to remain close to Lisbon so as to maintain the illusion that the French army was blockading Wellington's troops. So he chose to retreat the army to Santarem, about 75 km from Lisbon up the River Tagus. From there, the French army could better feed itself and still be able to threaten the Anglo-Portuguese army north of Lisbon.

On 14 November, the French army started to withdraw from the Lines of Torres Vedras. By 18 November it was posted in Santarem, Tomar and Punhete, forming a triangular perimeter. It was a strong position that would be hard to attack or outflank. Masséna hoped that Wellington would mount an assault, but Wellington certainly never fell for such an obvious trap. Instead, he deployed his troops to 'confine' the French as much as possible without engaging in 'any serious affair' with the enemy. He thus had about 48,000 troops watching Masséna's army in the Santarem perimeter of some 46,800 men. Over 9,000 of Masséna's men were detached and nearly 19,000 were listed as sick.

As ordered by Napoleon, General Drouet D'Erlon did move the 20,700 men of his 9th Corps into Almeida in mid-November and then towards Masséna so as to keep communications open. This was not an easy task, and only strong detachments could hope to do the job in the very hostile countryside that ran from Ciudad Rodrigo in Spain to Santarem. Drouet had to leave numerous detachments along the way, notably General Clarapède's Division of nearly 9,000 men at Guarda. Even so, there was little protection from Don Julian Sanchez's mounted guerrillas or Silveira's levies. All the detachments left only some 7,500 men of General Conroux's Division at Leiria to reinforce Masséna's army, which was without doubt inadequate. To make matters worse, widespread sickness broke out in Drouet's 9th Corps so that by March 1811, Clarapède's Division had shrunk to 6,000 and Conroux's to 6,500. In southern Spain, Soult was much too busy fighting the Spanish in the area of Granada to immediately move to Portugal's border. He was also reluctant to lose part of his Andalucian domain for the sake of helping Masséna. He eventually moved west with 20,000 men to take Badajos from the Spanish in January 1811. While this move would not save the French in Portugal, it did consolidate Soult's own position in southern Spain.

Northern Movements

The Portuguese forces opposing the French in the north were largely irregular troops. In the area north and northwest of Almeida was General Silveira commanding the reformed 24th Infantry with six embodied militia regiments, Wilson with four militia battalions at Viseu and Trant with seven battalions at Coimbra. General Manuel Bacelar, commander in chief in northern Portugal, was at Porto. Silveira's command was the closest to the French line of communication but he had given up the blockade of Almeida when the 9th Corps arrived there. Badly outnumbered, the Portuguese troops had gone to Trancoso and then evacuated it when General Clarapède marched there with his division in late December 1810. Silveira retreated further while keeping contact with the pursuing French. General Bacelar instructed his

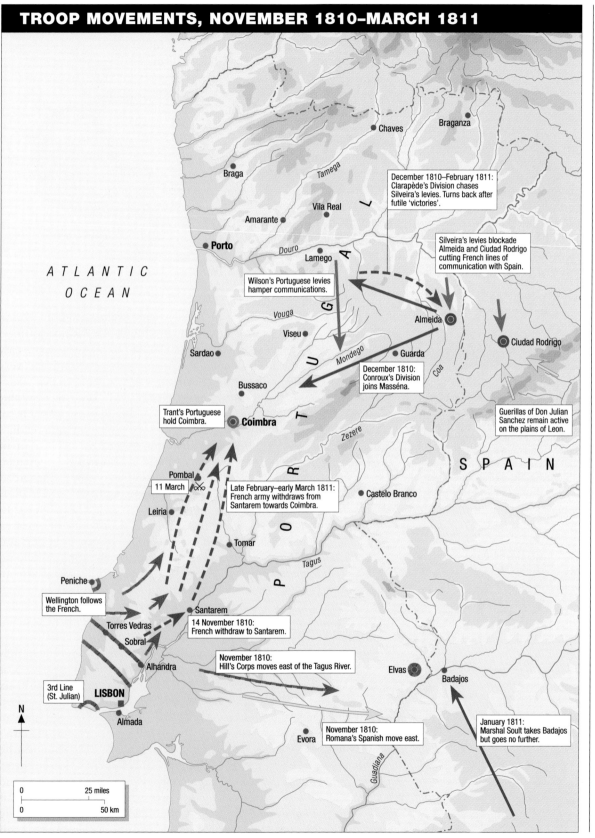

Chaves

Braganza

Braga

Tamega

Vila Real

Amarante

December 1810–February 1811:
Clarapède's Division chases
Silveira's levies. Turns back after
futile 'victories'.

Porto

Douro

Lamego

Silveira's levies blockade
Almeida and Ciudad Rodrigo
cutting French lines of
communication with Spain.

Wilson's Portuguese levies
hamper communications.

ATLANTIC
OCEAN

Vouga

Viseu

Almeida

Ciudad Rodrigo

Sardao

Mondego

Guarda

Coa

December 1810:
Conroux's Division
joins Masséna.

Bussaco

Trant's Portuguese
hold Coimbra.

Coimbra

Zezere

Guerillas of Don Julian
Sanchez remain active
on the plains of Leon.

S P A I N

Pombal

11 March

Late February–early March 1811:
French army withdraws from
Santarem towards Coimbra.

Leiria

Castelo Branco

Tomar

Tagus

Peniche

Wellington follows
the French.

Santarem

Torres Vedras

14 November 1810:
French withdraw to Santarem.

Sobral

Alhandra

November 1810:
Hill's Corps moves east of the Tagus River.

Elvas

Badajos

**3rd Line
(St. Julian)**

LISBON

Almada

N

November 1810:
Romana's Spanish move east.

Evora

January 1811:
Marshal Soult takes Badajos
but goes no further.

Guadiana

0   25 miles

0   50 km

P O R T U G A L

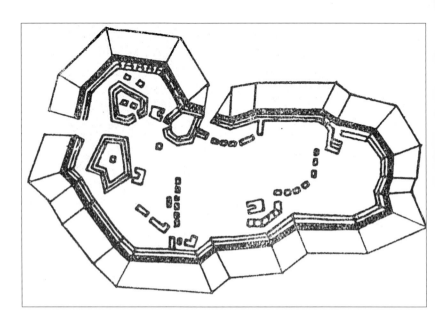

commanders to keep an eye on the French while avoiding action. At this time, Conroux's Division was marching west along the Mondego River while Clarapède's was going towards Viseu so that Bacelar was unsure as to the French objective. If the target was the city of Porto, it was the only place that Bacelar felt worth defending and where a strong stand could be attempted. Should the French troop movement towards Porto be confirmed, Silveira, Trant and Wilson were to take their troops there to join others gathering from elsewhere.

In the event, Drouet with Conroux's Division turned south towards Masséna. This still left Clarapède's Division at Trancoso, which was constantly shadowed by Silveira's troops. On 30 December, Clarapède attacked Silveira's Portuguese at Ponte de Abbade, south of Lamego, and made them retreat after inflicting about 200 casualties. Another French sortie, on 11 January 1811, caught Silveira off guard and his shaken irregulars fled, some all the way to Lamego on the Douro River. It was a serious blow but it did not cripple the Portuguese forces. Bacelar ordered a concentration of Trant's and other troops at Castro d'Aire so that by January 1811, some 14,000 Portuguese troops of all sorts had gathered there. Clarapède was getting worried as he was sure his 6,000 men would soon be vastly outnumbered and, on about 22 January, he retreated his division from Trancoso back to Colerico and Guarda with Silveira's men following close behind. Thus, by February, the situation was about the same as two months earlier in spite of Clarapède's manoeuvrings and 'victories' which proved hollow. The French were again basically surrounded in Guarda, Colerico and Almeida with Silveira's levies keeping an eye on them. The road was still no safer for French couriers and only those with a strong escort could be confident of getting through.[15]

Further south, Wellington kept watch on Masséna's troops around Santarem and the reinforcements that arrived in Leiria with part of the 6th Corps. These new troops helped keep Trant's Portuguese militias at bay in the north while the French foraged and seized whatever food they could find in this relatively less ravaged area of the country. But it took only a few weeks before the area was stripped of any supplies, and nourishment for men and horses once again became a persistent problem. In Santarem, hidden food supplies had been found, but these too would eventually run out with no replenishments in sight.

Wellington had also detached General Rowland Hill with his 2nd Division and two Portuguese brigades to the east bank of the Tagus in late November 1810. Hill's force was ordered to check any French force advancing on that area from Santarem or from southern Spain. In late November, Hill became very sick and Wellington replaced him in early December with Marshal Beresford, the commander of the Portuguese army. He commanded the Allied forces to the east of the Tagus River. The Spanish corps went to Olivenza on the border with Spain to confront Soult's movements in that area. Unfortunately, on 23 January 1811, General the Marquis of Romana, who commanded the Spanish corps, unexpectedly died of a sudden illness depriving Wellington of one of the very few Spanish generals he trusted. The situation remained stable on the Spanish border as Marshal Soult did not attempt to move into Portugal.

By February, Masséna realised that staying in Santarem to renew an attack on Lisbon was all but hopeless. Food and forage were scarce and the promised reinforcements more modest than hoped and certainly not sufficient for offensive operations against a strong enemy. His foe, Wellington, could not be lured into an attack on unfavourable ground and was, as a general officer, making very few tactical mistakes. On 16 February, Masséna met with his three corps commanders to outline a retreat back to Spain to the northeast. Almeida would be held while the army would concentrate at Ciudad Rodrigo. Marshal Ney objected, arguing that the best course was to withdraw east and join Soult's army on the Spanish border. Junot felt that a bridgehead on the east bank of the Tagus would preserve a certain presence in Portugal and eventually provide a base for a future attack on Lisbon. Reynier, the least talented tactician, had the worst plan which split the army in two. Masséna prevailed and the decision to retreat to the northeast was confirmed.

12 A letter by the Duke of Wellington to his brother William Wellesley-Pole, edited by Sir Charles Webster, *Camden Miscellany*, Vol. XVIII (London, 1948), p.34. Wellington was certainly feeling optimistic and went on to ask his brother to have two good horses sent to him, stating that the 'Irish Hack Hunter with good feet & Legs & shoulders is the best of any for Service. Never mind the price.'

13 D'Urban's Journal, 3–6 November 1810. General Silveira had good intelligence from Spain and reported French troop movements of 2,000 men from Salamanca to Ciudad Rodrigo which was received at the Allied army HQ on 8 November. However, D'Urban, who was the Quartermaster General of the Portuguese army (from 1809 to 1817), did not like Silveira although we are not told why. On looking at Silveira's record during the Peninsular War and at his personal conduct throughout his life, D'Urban's animosity seems misplaced.

14 *Mémoires du Maréchal Marmont Duc de Raguse* (Paris, 1857), Vol. IV. Although Marmont took over command from Masséna on 11 May 1811, he was obviously briefed in great detail on the previous conduct of Masséna's army.

15 William F.P. Napier, *History of the War in the Peninsula and in Southern France*, Vol. II, book XII, violently criticised Silveira as a vain and 'insufficient' commander in these operations. Portuguese historian Luz Soriano, *Historia da Guerra Civil*, Vol. III, p.277, vigorously defended Silveira by recalling his excellent record against what he considered to be slander by Napier. The author feels Napier's comments were regrettable as they were obviously unfounded considering the general result of the operations.

MASSÉNA'S RETREAT

O n 6 March, Allied scouts confirmed that Santarem was empty and Wellington occupied the place the same day. Nearby bridges had been blown up, Junot's and Reynier's rearguard corps were already far away. Wellington sent the Light Division and Pack's Brigade to follow them. He was still suspicious that Masséna might be trying to lure him into a trap but the following days and weeks confirmed that the French army was indeed retreating. The Anglo-Portuguese did not pursue the French closely, as Wellington wished only to follow the French and not to provoke a fight.

Another factor slowing the pursuit was the utterly ruinous state of the Portuguese towns and countryside that the Allied troops encountered. What little food and forage it might have contained had been plundered by the starved French for the last three months. All the rations and forage on which the Allied army depended had, therefore, to be transported from Lisbon. The desolation the British and Portuguese soldiers found in towns and hamlets recently vacated by the French was almost beyond belief. Santarem was a town of vandalised and half-destroyed houses. Filth and dead animals lay in the streets alongside the smashed remnants of fine furniture piled up as firewood. The villages lay in ruins, many buildings containing the remains of the unfortunate peasants who had stayed behind.[16]

North or Northeast?

As the French army marched north, Wellington instructed the commanders of the Portuguese militia corps, who would be faced with Masséna's troops, to withdraw rather than fight. Not only would these irregulars be no match for the French veterans but both Wilson's and Trant's corps only amounted to about 6,000 troops.

As Wellington became convinced that Masséna was indeed leading his troops out of Portugal rather than staging some sort of feint, he pressed the pursuit more closely. Wellington had around 46,000 men, including 14,000 Portuguese to follow the French. The army consisted of the 1st, 3rd, 4th, 5th and 6th divisions, Pack's and Ashworth's Portuguese brigades with some cavalry and artillery. The new 7th Division, 5,100 strong, was being formed in Lisbon and not yet with Wellington's Allied army. Wilson and Trant's corps operating around Coimbra and in the country to the north amounted to only about 6,000 militiamen. They were not capable of facing the French army and were ordered to withdraw to Porto if the French marched on Coimbra.

Masséna's army retreated in three columns under Reynier, Junot and Ney. In all, some 49,000 men marched north towards Coimbra. It was possible that Masséna would continue north and attempt to take Porto. Both Wellington and General Bacelar, the Portuguese commander in

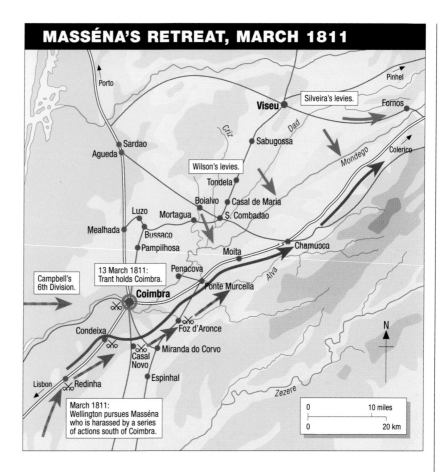

MASSÉNA'S RETREAT, MARCH 1811

Porto

Pinhel

Viseu

Silveira's levies.

Fornos

Criz

Sabugossa

Dad

Sardao

Colerico

Agueda

Mondego

Wilson's levies.

Tondela

Boialvo · Casal de Maria

Luzo

Mortagua

S. Combadao

Mealhada

Bussaco

Pampilhosa

Moita

Chamusca

Penacova

13 March 1811:
Trant holds Coimbra.

Campbell's
6th Division.

Ponte Murcella

Alva

Coimbra

N

Foz d'Aronce

Condeixa

Miranda do Corvo

Casal
Novo

Espinhal

Lisbon · Redinha

Zezere

March 1811:
Wellington pursues Masséna
who is harassed by a series
of actions south of Coimbra.

0   10 miles

0   20 km

the area, knew the Portuguese could not resist such an assault. Wellington hoped that if they were closely pursued, the retreating French would be more inclined to head for the relative safety of the Almeida and Ciudad Rodrigo area in western Spain than to risk operations against Porto. Masséna faced the possibility of being caught between Wellington's troops behind him and an untold number of Portuguese troops entrenched around Porto. However, if the pursuit relaxed Masséna may feel he had enough time to seize Porto. The 3,000 Allied cavalrymen, 500 of whom were Portuguese and the rest British or German, pursued the French relentlessly, closely followed by the Light Division.

As the French neared Coimbra on 10 March, Masséna considered crossing the Mondego River to take it. He was hesitant, however, as intelligence had reached him that General Silveira's troops had joined Trant's in the city. The French believed that some 15,000 to 20,000 Portuguese troops were dug in defending the city. This was not the case at all. Although Trant and his Portuguese militia brigade remained in the city, they were, as per Wellington's instructions, ready to retreat at the first sustained French attempt. There was no point in sacrificing Trant's men. Heavy rains had caused the river to rise, making a crossing difficult while the British light troops to the south were catching up and skirmishing with the French rearguard. The next day a sharp skirmish occurred in Pombal in which the Allied Light Division and Picton's 3rd Division clashed with Marshal Ney's 6th Corps. British

Windmill south of Sobral. This may have been the windmill from where Marshal Masséna surveyed the first line of Torres Vedras on 14 October 1810. (Photo: RC)

riflemen and Portuguese Cazadores pressed the French rearguard. Marshal Ney was, as always, at his best in combat, however, and quickly had a column drive the Allied vanguard back. The French rescued some troops stranded in Pombal's old castle and fired part of the town. By this time the French were engaged with the 3rd, 4th and Light divisions and Ney withdrew his men. French losses at 63 were nevertheless nearly double those of the Allies at 37.

At Coimbra, Trant's cannon were exchanging fire with French horse artillery across the river. The French generals were concerned that their army might be caught with its back to the Mondego River, trapped between the Portuguese in Coimbra and Wellington's army. Part of Wellington's army, indeed, catching up with the French at Redinha, a town about 25 km south of Coimbra where a sizeable French rearguard was posted. It now seemed to Masséna that the wiser course was to forget about Coimbra and Porto and head east towards Spain. In a rather hasty move, Masséna sent Drouet with Conroux's Division of the 9th Corps east towards Spain with instructions to contact Clarapède's Division in the Colerico area. Masséna's instinct to re-establish communications was sensible enough, but the effect was to weaken his army by some 5,000 men precisely when it was fighting off the pursuing Allied troops.

REDINHA, CONDEIXA, CASAL NOVO AND FOZ D'ARONCE

Wellington was indeed pursuing; on 12 March his Light, 3rd and 4th divisions and Pack's Brigade reached Redinha close behind Julien Mermet's rearguard division of Ney's 6th Corps. Ney had also detached the 3rd Hussars, a few dragoon squadrons and eight guns. Wellington was cautious as his scouts had reported another French column about 8 km east, and that stragglers and invalids from Junot's 8th Corps had been captured in the area. At about midday, the Light and 4th divisions, Pack's Brigade and the 3rd Division were deployed from west to east in

ABOVE **The medieval castle of Sao Vincente overlooking Torres Vedras. In 1810, it was one of the main redoubts of the lines. (Photo: RC)**

LEFT **The battle of Redinha, 12 March 1811. This picture shows British light dragoons attacking French dragoons but the engagement was largely an infantry battle. (Print after Martinet)**

a line facing Mermet. With the Allied 1st and 6th divisions marching up the road from the south, Wellington's force was much stronger than Ney's, and at 2.00pm the British and Portuguese line advanced. Mermet's flanks were turned by the Light Division to the west and Picton's 3rd Division to the east. The fighting was intense but Ney knew that Mermet's troops would have to withdraw or be overwhelmed. He had consequently instructed the colour party of each unit to fall back to positions 3 km north at the foot of a ridge where a new defence line would be formed. At Ney's order, Mermet's line withdrew in echelon to

The centre of the city of Torres Vedras. The castle of Sao Vincente is on top of the hill. (Photo: RC)

The fortress of Peniche on the seacoast north of the Lines of Torres Vedras remained in Anglo-Portuguese possession and posed a menace to Masséna's northwestern flank. (Photo: RC)

the new position. The French soldiers ran back in good order until they got to the narrow bridge over the Ancos River at the back of Redinha where something of a traffic jam occurred. Allied skirmishers had already reached the vicinity of the bridge and peppered the French who were crossing it. But other French troops were also crossing at pre-identified fords in the river. Picton tried to outflank Mermet to cut off his retreat but the move failed and the French deployed in their new position. It took some time for the Allied troops to cross and form a new line in front of the French. When, once again, Ney felt he was about to be overwhelmed, he gave the order to withdraw. It was now evening, and the British and Portuguese vanguard pursued the French some distance, but again Ney drew up two battalions in a double line on a ridge which poured a heavy fire on the Allied troops before retreating in good order. The French suffered 227 casualties and the Allies 205 but Ney had achieved his objectives; he had protected the rear of the army, his own corps rearguard had been safely withdrawn and Wellington had been delayed by a day.

On 13 March, Ney's 6th Corps was deployed at Condeixa, about 12 km north, where the road was flanked by hills and afforded a good defensive position. The countryside was becoming increasingly mountainous as the armies moved north. Wellington used the same deployment as at Redinha, but this time the 3rd Division outflanked the French by making a detour through a mountain pass to the east, while the 6th Division did the same to the west. As a result, Ney became aware of a trickle of enemy troops appearing behind both flanks. There was no time to lose and he signalled a retreat lest his two divisions be caught, setting fire to Condeixa as he fell back hastily with Picton's 3rd Division close behind. Only Ney's speedy response allowed this narrow escape. The 6th Corps settled in at Casal Novo.

In the early evening, a curious incident occurred that was indicative of the closeness of the pursuit. A forward patrol of King's German Legion hussars was already close to Fonte Cuberta, a village between Condeixa and Casal Novo, when it chanced upon a large party of French officers dining under the shade of a tree just outside the entrance to the village. Both sides were startled and the hussars hesitated, wondering what they had stumbled upon. At the same time some 50 French dragoons who were nearby ran to mount their horses. The Legion hussars had disturbed Marshal Masséna and his staff at dinner! A few grenadiers on guard formed up to protect Masséna, while the dragoons, who were Masséna's escort, and some Aides de Camp prepared to charge the hussars. Meanwhile, Masséna and the other officers escaped in the opposite direction. Marbot, who was present, stated that if the '50 English hussars' had charged immediately, they could have killed, wounded or captured Masséna.

In the event, Masséna reached Loison's Division close by and blamed Ney for not covering the position with pickets. Ney had been dealing with Wellington's intricate manoeuvres and had warned Masséna that he

The fortress of Almada across the narrow entrance of the Tagus River guarded Lisbon's southern flank. It was refurbished and garrisoned with Lisbon volunteers in 1810–11.

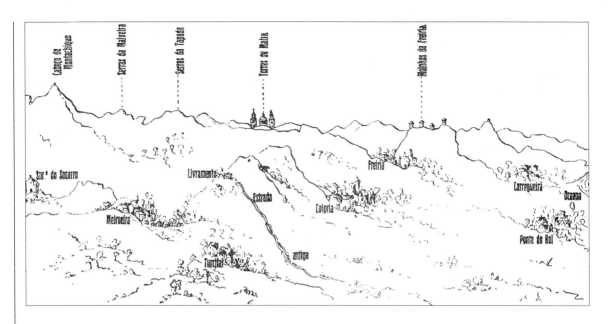

Cabeço de Montachique — Serras da Malveira — Serras da Tapada — Torres de Mafra — Ridinhas da Freiria

Snr.ª de Socorro — Livramento — Estrada — Freiria — Carregueira — Ozana

Melrocha — Colorin — antiga — Ponte do Rol

Turcifal

A view of the towns on the second line of Torres Vedras looking towards the southeast. The Atlantic Ocean is at right. The towers of the town of Mafra are at the centre in the distance. The topography as shown in this print is somewhat exaggerated.

was withdrawing, however, the ADC with the message got lost and reached Masséna hours later. Some staff officers sympathetic to Masséna suspected Ney never actually sent a courier, which gives some indication of the extent to which relations had deteriorated between the two marshals.

The French continued to suffer from inadequate intelligence. Alexander Campbell's 6th Division was operating separately from Wellington's main force and was west of Coimbra by 13 March. The French scouts believed this was a new body of troops that had been landed by ship to join Wellington's army. Coupled with the belief that there were substantial forces in Coimbra, this confirmed Masséna's belief that retiring to Spain was the prudent option.

Early on 14 March, the British and Portuguese vanguard under Sir William Erskine ran into General Marchand's French rearguard at Casal Novo. The fighting started in the early morning fog and the French held on until the fog lifted, by which time the five battalions of the Light Division were advancing, supported by the 3rd Division. Marchand withdrew to a second position further back which was eventually also vacated after some determined fighting. It was a fine rearguard action as Marchand's men inflicted 155 casualties while losing a relatively modest 55 killed or wounded themselves.

The French army was heading northeast to take the main road leading to Colerico and, ultimately, the fortress of Almeida and Ciudad Rodrigo in Spain. Perhaps because of the incident with the German hussars, Masséna was keen to speed up the retreat. With their army approaching the mountains and the Anglo-Portuguese army closing on them from behind, the French urgently needed to lighten their load as much as possible. All wheeled transports including marshals' carriages were destroyed, with the exception of some ammunition wagons. Many of the horses and donkeys were slaughtered although a number were still alive, wallowing in the mud when the British came up. It was a useless and barbaric act according to Grattan of the 52nd and Donaldson of the 94th, as the poor creatures were exhausted and of no use to the Allied army, which had sufficient numbers of good mules.

The mansion of the Baron of Manique where Wellington had his HQ at Pero Negro in the autumn of 1810. (Photo: RC)

Another worry during the retreat for Masséna was his mistress, Madame X. Now riding a horse, she fell several times as her mount stumbled over rocks in the darkness and she became so weak that she could no longer walk, having to be carried by a few sturdy grenadiers of Masséna's escort. While asking his staff officers not to abandon her, he confided several times: 'what an error I made in bringing a woman to war.'[17]

By 15 March, the French had reached Foz d'Aronce, indeed their 2nd Corps had passed it. Wellington was in close pursuit. Here another stand was made by the French, with Marchand's and half of Mermet's divisions of Ney's 6th Corps once again deployed in front of the town, and Junot's 8th Corps with the other half of Mermet's Division on a ridge just beyond the Ceira River behind the town. There had been heavy fog earlier that day but by 4.00pm it had cleared, although Ney – who once again was in charge of the rearguard – did not expect an attack. Wellington on the contrary, saw this as an opportunity and pressed on. Picton's 3rd Division and the Light Divisions were ordered to attack while Pack went west to outflank the French position. Once again, Mermet's troops defended their ground with courage but lost heavily, finally blowing up the bridge over the Ceira in their retreat. French losses were heavy at about 250 while the Allied troops reported 71, a third of which were suffered by the 95th Rifles when a few companies of that unit broke through the French centre position. Wellington did not want to go any further; his men were exhausted and most of Masséna's army could be seen on the hills beyond the Ceira River.

MARCHING EAST

The next morning, 16 March, the hills were bare and the French army gone. Only a few small French detachments were visible. Curiously, Wellington seemed less anxious to pursue, which may have puzzled some of his officers as well as the enemy. Until this point Wellington could not be sure that Masséna, that 'sly old fox', would not try to storm Coimbra

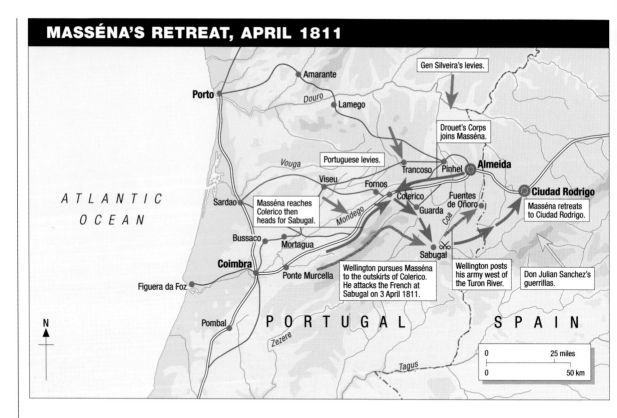

and march on Porto. Now, however, after this series of skirmishes, he had the satisfaction of knowing that Masséna was retreating towards the Spanish frontier. This must have given great joy to not only his British officers but also the Portuguese officers. A few days later, Wellington instructed that most of the militiamen and Ordenanza on duty at the Torres Vedras lines and other defences around Lisbon should be sent home. The crisis, which had begun with the invasion of Portugal in July 1810, was over.

The campaign, however, was far from over. Wellington's army followed the French closely on their march towards Colerico along the main road south of the Mondego River. To discourage French raids and marauders, Trant's and Wilson's Portuguese militia brigades shadowed the French along the north bank of the Mondego. In the following days, hundreds of French deserters and stragglers were gathered by British and Portuguese troops as Masséna's ragged army marched east. Some were also captured, notably General Loison's ADC and his wife by a party of the 95th Rifles on 19 March.[18] Finally, after many incidents, the French army reached the town of Colerico and united with Drouet's 9th Corps. The worst may have seemed over to French soldiers, but further misfortune awaited.

On 22 March, Masséna issued orders that shocked the army to its core. Until then it had been understood the army would retreat into western Spain via Almeida. Now, with Almeida almost in sight, Masséna suddenly decided to march the army to Guarda instead, then south across the mountains into Spanish Estramadura. He then aimed to march back into Portugal again and occupy the upper Tagus River. Masséna's wild scheme, plucked out of thin air, took no account of the

state of the Army of Portugal – it was exhausted, lacking clothing, shoes and would soon lack food. It was also still being pursued by Wellington.

Marshal Ney's Dismissal

For Marshal Ney this was the last straw. In his opinion the army needed rest, clothing and food, which it could only get by marching to Almeida and into Spain. He could not bear to see his 6th Corps, which he had raised and served with since 1804, taken on such an adventure and announced that he was taking his corps to Almeida. His rage was incandescent and, on 22 March, he wrote three letters to Masséna within a few hours stating his position. This was gross insubordination and Masséna responded by relieving Ney from command. The army was shocked to see its favourite commander turned out by the unpopular Masséna. Had Ney refused to obey as some officers wished, the 6th Corps and perhaps the whole army might have taken his side. But he was not that kind of general. He obeyed Masséna and left for France. The command of the 6th Corps was given to General Loison.[19]

As events demonstrated, Masséna's wild plan proved impossible to execute. By 27 March, both generals Reynier and Junot wrote to Masséna that their corps were close to starving, as there were no food or supplies to be had in the desolate and mountainous country further south. A day later, Masséna concluded that the only way out was to march east into Spain.

Napoleon's interview with
General Foy on 22 November
1810 regarding the French
army's campaign in Portugal.

With Wellington's army not far behind, the French continued their retreat. They tarried a little in Guarda and by 29 March, two Allied cavalry brigades, the 3rd, 6th and Light divisions were in the town's vicinity. They ran into Mermet's, Marchand's and Ferey's divisions. Their commander, General Loison, was an able general, but he lacked the outstanding tactical ability of Marshal Ney, and he was taken by surprise as the Anglo-Portuguese troops arrived in Guarda, which his 6th Corps left in a hurry, trading shots with the Allied soldiers. On 31 March, the French crossed the Coa River. Masséna's army had shrunk to less than 40,000 men during the retreat but now added the 4,500 men of Clarapède's Division of 9th Corps posted around Almeida. He therefore decided to make a stand on the east side of the Coa in the area of Sabugal, about 30 km south of Almeida.

SABUGAL

Even allowing for recently arrived reinforcements, with 38,000 men Wellington's army was still smaller than Masséna's, although this number did not include Pack's Portuguese Brigade further west nor Trant's and Wilson's levies of irregulars who were on the north bank of the Mondego River. Wellington's plan was to outflank Masséna from the south while Trant and Wilson's Portuguese militias crossed the Coa River to threaten

the French northern flank around Almeida. Drouet's 9th Corps was thus preoccupied on that front, while the French 6th and 8th corps were strung out further south with the 2nd Corps somewhat isolated at Sabugal. Retaining the initiative, Wellington marched eastwards and, at the beginning of April, was in sight of Sabugal. The 6th Allied Division faced the French 6th Corps across the Coa River keeping Loison suitably worried while Wellington moved five divisions, some 30,000 men, to attack Sabugal and, he hoped, wipe out Reynier's 2nd Corps. In the event Reynier was lucky, the Allies attacked on the morning of 3 April amidst a dense fog, which helped conceal their movements but proved very confusing. The 3rd and 5th Allied divisions decided not to advance blindly and asked Wellington for further orders. Not so General Esrkine, who commanded the Light Division. Without bothering to see the terrain himself, he sent an ADC to order the division and the cavalry to cross the river at previously identified fords. In the confusion the Light Division crossed at the wrong place, much closer to Sabugal than planned. The cavalry, taking its cue from the Light Division, was looking for a non-existent ford even further from its correct position, everyone was more or less lost in the fog. The French piquets of Reynier's 2nd Corps on the east side of the river heard all this movement, and when they saw elements of Beckwith's Brigade crossing the river, they opened a heavy fire. They were rapidly driven off by the men of the 43rd, 95th and the 3rd Cazadores, however, and the brigade formed up and marched on. Still in the fog, it ran into the 4th French Light Infantry Regiment as they were forming up, and they too were driven off. Additional troops from Pierre Merle's Division were arriving, however, and soon, seven French battalions faced Beckwith's Brigade. Rain now began to pour reducing the firepower of both sides. Beckwith, realising he was outnumbered and seeing no relief anywhere in the mist and rain, made for a nearby hill. Capturing a howitzer in the process, the 1,500 men of the brigade formed in a desperate stand on the slopes facing some 3,500 Frenchmen. Fortunately for Beckwith, the 2,000 men of the Light Division's 2nd Brigade under Colonel Charles Drummond arrived on the scene, marching through the fog to the sound of the guns. The 52nd, 1st Cazadores and four companies of the 95th Rifles deployed and much

Map of the battle of Sabugal on 3 April 1811. One must bear in mind that this engagement was fought in a blinding fog with rain falling. The situation shown is during the latter part of the battle when the fog lifted. The British cavalry being somewhere south of the Coa River as a result of Erskine's orders, the French slipped away to the west. The Anglo-Portuguese are shown in red, the French in green. (Luz Soriano, III)

confused fighting took place in the mist and rain. More French troops came up and at one point two French cavalry squadrons charged but, by chance, a squadron of the British 16th Light Dragoons arrived and helped drive them off. The British troopers had lost their way and headed for the gunfire. Erskine was by now totally confused and his orders ultimately prevented the rest of the cavalry from joining the battle.

Neither Wellington nor Reynier had any idea of what was going on, although the former guessed that little was going according to plan. The fog then lifted and he saw through the rain the bulk of the Light Division facing masses of French troops and their northern flank being turned by a French column. The spectacle was far from encouraging, but Reynier had little cause for joy as he could see the 3rd and 5th Allied divisions crossing the Coa River. Many thousands more Anglo-Portuguese troops would shortly join the fight. His corps would inevitably be crushed and Reynier immediately ordered a general retreat off to the east. Masséna's line on the Coa River was pierced and in the afternoon the French army withdrew towards Spain.

The immensely destructive third invasion of Portugal, which had started in the summer of 1810, was over. But the threat of renewed invasion remained, and the French still held the strategic fortress of Almeida.

---

16 Sergeant Edward Costello of the 95th Rifles related a particularly grim incident when a Cazadore of the Light Division found the bayoneted and 'mangled bodies' of his parents, just murdered 'their blood still warm', and of his only sister 'breathing her last, and exhibiting dreadful proofs of the brutality with which she had been violated.' The cazadore, blinded with grief, saw French prisoners nearby and killed one and wounded another before being overcome by their guards and taken prisoner. He was later liberated when the circumstances became known to the commanding general. This sad incident nevertheless demonstrates that the Allied army took measures to protect French prisoners from wanton vengeance. The French treated the British prisoners with respect but not the Portuguese and Spanish.

17 Marbot, Vol. II, p.435. Marbot also mentioned that Marshal Ney could not stand Madame X and would not dine with Masséna if she was present.

18 John Kinkaid, *Adventures in the Rifle Brigade* (London, 1830), p. 62. The ADC was described as 'a Portuguese, and a traitor, and looked very like a man who would be hanged' while his wife 'who was dressed in a splendid hussar uniform … was a Spaniard, and very handsome, and looked like a woman who would get married again.'

19 Masséna immediately sent Colonel Jean-Jacques Pelet, his ADC, to Paris so his version would be heard first by the emperor. When Ney got to Paris, he was gently admonished by Napoleon and then given further important commands. On Loison, see Campaign 90 *Vimeiro 1808*.

THE BATTLE OF FUENTES DE OÑORO 3–5 MAY 1811

At the end of March 1811, Napoleon sent instructions that the HQ of the Army of Portugal should remain in Coimbra until it attacked Lisbon! How different was the reality facing the French army. It was a long way from Coimbra and had just left Guarda. Masséna retreated just across the Spanish border, finding himself back where he had started some ten months earlier. His campaign seemed to have been totally fruitless. Many men of the Army of Portugal had been lost at the battle of Bussaco and from exposure in the following months, while unable to pierce the Lines of Torres Vedras, drive the British into the sea and take Lisbon at last. The single, solitary French gain in Portugal had been the fortress of Almeida.

Wellington was not far behind the French. Welcome news was that General Robert Craufurd was arriving from leave in England to resume command of his Light Division. Sir William Erskine had been a relatively competent division commander but, being somewhat unused to the rapid movements of light troops, it had been a difficult duty for him whereas Craufurd was an outstanding light troops general. The news was greeted by all as a good omen for the army as it neared the Spanish border.

Wellington surrounds Almeida

Once again, the fortress of Almeida was to play a key role in dictating the course of the campaign. Masséna knew that if he could retain control of Almeida, the Anglo-Portuguese army would be unable to threaten the French hold on western Spain whilst leaving such a powerful enemy base uncaptured in their rear. The French marshal had no intention of keeping his whole army there, as the fortress would probably be surrounded and, in any event, the Spanish plains of Leon would be a better source of food and supplies than the rocky hills of Portugal. The countryside surrounding Almeida, Guarda and Sebugal was devastated and Masséna's army was critically short of food, forage and all sorts of supplies – a rather sorry-looking shadow of the splendid and confident force that had crossed into Portugal the previous year. He therefore left a strong force in Almeida and his army then fell back towards Ciudad Rodrigo.

Almeida had been partly destroyed by a catastrophic explosion on 26 August 1810 which had led to its surrender to the French and opened the route into Portugal. By drafting labourers the French garrison had, eight months later, made enough repairs to once again make the fortress a mighty obstacle. General Antoine-François Brenier, a tough and experienced veteran, was left as governor of the fortress with a garrison of about 1,300 troops.

Wellington's troops reached the area in April, and the 6th Division with Pack's Portuguese Brigade surrounded Almeida. The other divisions and brigades were spread between Almeida and Concepcion. The Light and 5th divisions were at the ruins of Fort Concepcion on the Spanish border acting as the vanguard of Wellington's army and watching Masséna. Provisions were quite scarce for the Anglo-Portuguese too, and not much could be expected in desolate villages such as Nava de Aver, Pozo Bello or Fuentes de Oñoro, but their commissariat was bringing in enough to sustain the men if not always all the animals. It would have to do for the time being. Wellington had no plans to march into the plains of Leon towards Ciudad Rodrigo. To do so, he believed, would expose his army to a counter-attack by a much stronger French force, as he was convinced that French troops in Spain would reinforce Masséna's army.

Wellington's hunch proved correct. Marshal Bessières, commander of the 70,000-man French 'Army of the North' in Spain was instructed to help his colleague Masséna prevent the British and Portuguese from entering Spain. Bessières was also supposed to be conducting operations against the remnants of the Spanish army in Galicia, however, and was further preoccupied by the intractable guerrilla problem, which required considerable forces to guard strategic points and communication routes. It may well have been Bessières's intense dislike of Masséna that, in the end, led him to state that all his troops were spoken for and only 1,600 cavalry and a battery of artillery were available.

Wellington, well informed as ever, therefore felt any immediate action by the French was unlikely, given the present state of their armies. He took the opportunity to make a lightning visit to the south. Accompanied by a few staff officers on good horses, he galloped south from Villar Formoso to the fortress of Elvas in five days, arriving there on 20 April, inspected troops and issued orders and then galloped north again, reaching his army at Alameda, a small village between the fortress of Almeida and Ciudad Rodrigo, on the 29th. It was an amazing feat that puzzled French intelligence officers.

MASSÉNA'S LAST CHANCE

Meanwhile, a mortified Napoleon sitting in Paris could only conclude, no doubt with some anguish, that Masséna who had up until then been one of his better marshals, was now a broken man. Following General Foy's reports he was left in no doubt. There was no alternative, and on 20 April Napoleon signed a letter relieving Masséna of command. Marshal Marmont, who had recently returned to France after a period of command in Dalmatia on the Adriatic, had been ordered to Spain to command 6th Corps following Marshal Ney's departure. While en route Marmont received the news that Masséna was dismissed and that he would take over command of the entire Army of Portugal rather than just 6th Corps.

Until Marshal Marmont reached the army in western Spain, Masséna remained in command. The French troops, except for the garrison of Almeida, were posted east of the Agueda River and in the area of Ciudad Rodrigo. Although Masséna was not yet aware of his dismissal, he knew he had failed in everything he was supposed to accomplish and that it could not be far off. However, reinforcements, supplies, clothing and ammunition were now reaching him as he could draw on the Army of Portugal reserves still in Spain. Up to 18,000 of these fresh troops were in the Salamanca area and thousands were marched west at once to replace the sick and worn out as well as to reinforce the battalions of the 2nd, 6th and 8th corps. Also in western Spain was General Drouet's 9th Corps, from which battalions were drawn to reinforce Masséna. Drouet was somewhat reluctant to do this but had no choice in the matter as the commanding officer in the area was Masséna. Thus, in spite of shortages in cavalry horses and in artillery, Masséna was rapidly re-establishing a formidable force, which by 1 May was already 42,000 strong.

Masséna's main concern was that Almeida should not fall to the Anglo-Portuguese. He had stated that it was a matter of honour that the fortress be held, but the strategic consequences were far more important if Almeida resisted. Masséna aimed to finally defeat Wellington in a general engagement. In this area there were no mountain ranges as at Bussaco and

no intricate fortifications such as those north of Lisbon to offer tactical advantages to Wellington and his men. If Masséna won the ensuing battle, and he felt his chances were great on such ground, the victory would vindicate him and, very likely, reinstate him in the emperor's favour.

He faced difficulties, however. His army was far from impressed with its commander-in-chief so far. His tactical imprudence, the amazing resilience of the enemy in Portugal, the shortages of all sorts notably in artillery, his disagreeable manner with other senior officers, his antics with his mistress Henriette Leberton, whom they knew as 'Madame X' and the shock of seeing the popular Marshal Ney dismissed, had badly shaken the respect and confidence the army should have had in its leader. Nevertheless, these reasons were not enough to deter French soldiers. Masséna had been a great general and might well regain his laurels if given the chance. A French army, even with low morale, was a fearsome, well-organised and hard-fighting entity whose spirit could quickly change from despair to the sublime if its men saw glimpses of glory – 'la gloire' – their ultimate inspiration. Masséna knew all this and knew he had a good chance to turn the tables on Wellington.

Wellington's Dispositions

On the Allied side, the forces available to Wellington were substantially weaker. Besides the troops blockading Almeida, he had about 37,000 men of whom a little over 10,000 were Portuguese, to face Masséna's rapidly growing force. The French outnumbered the Allies' 34,000 infantry by some 8,000 men. The Anglo-Portuguese were especially weak in cavalry with a mere 1,850 troopers, including 312 Portuguese, to face 4,500 French cavalry. Only in artillery did Wellington have superiority over Masséna, with four British and four Portuguese batteries totalling 48 guns against the French 38.

The French might well have had even more troops had it not been for the animosity between marshals Masséna and Bessières. Bessières commanded at Salamanca, and the sudden arrival of Masséna's 40,000 starving and ragged men from Portugal in his area had greatly strained both the supplies and personal relations already soured by jealousy and power struggles. Bessières sent rations for 20,000 men, which he felt was all

ABOVE **The village of Fuentes de Oñoro looking towards the east. The initial French attack on 3 May 1811 came from that direction. (Photo: RC)**

BELOW **Fuentes de Oñoro as seen from a bluff just southwest of the village. Wellington is likely to have been on that bluff as it offers a commanding view from high ground. (Photo: RC)**

he could spare, and further claimed all of his troops were tied up holding down guerrillas. This may have been true, but Masséna doubted it. As Bessières had promised to help Masséna contain the Anglo-Portuguese, he duly marched westward and joined Masséna with a small force consisting of 1,700 cavalry, half of which was detached from the Imperial Guard, and a battery of Imperial Guard horse artillery. Had Bessières been able to gather even 10,000 men, Wellington would have had to withdraw behind the Coa River. Fortunately for the Allied cause, he did not.

Wellington, who enjoyed excellent intelligence largely thanks to the Spanish guerrillas of Don Julian Sanchez, probably knew that he was outnumbered by 2 May, but not by enough enemy troops to warrant a retreat should the French advance to relieve Almeida. Wellington was in a fighting mood if, as ever, prudent.

If one had to pick the quality that most typically characterised Wellington, that quality could well be his remarkable eye for terrain. At first glance, as one nears the Spanish border from the west, the terrain appears to be fairly flat. However, reaching the small village of Fuentes de Oñoro, one notes it is built on a gentle slope just west of the narrow and shallow Dos Casas River. The ground just behind the hamlet is higher and open, stretching across a broad, low plateau until the River Coa is reached about 15 km further west. This meant that a force posted behind the village would have the advantage of higher ground as the flat plain to the east was somewhat lower. The nature of the ground around the village attracted Wellington's attention, and he saw it as a suitable place to meet a French attack. It was not perfect, as it would be exposed to enemy fire, but it had many sturdy stone walls and solid buildings. The village would also be difficult to outflank. Wellington took advantage of these various features, making Fuentes de Oñoro the southern flank of the Anglo-Portuguese army, guarded by Sir Brent Spencer's 1st Division.

To the northwest, in the vicinity of the village of Villar Formoso, were

Fuentes de Oñoro as seen from near the river. This is the view French soldiers would have had as they charged into the village. (Photo:

A street in Fuentes de Oñoro that was no doubt the scene of desperate fighting during the bloody battle in 1811. (Photo: RC)

Houston's 7th Division and Picton's 3rd Division. Further north was Campbell's 6th Division on the road midway between the villages of Alameda (not to be confused with the Fortress of Almeida further west) and Sao Pedro. Erskine's 5th Division was just below Aldea do Obispo near the ruined Fort Concepcion. Just to the north were some Portuguese cavalry piquets. Craufurd's Light Division with four regi-ments of cavalry was posted further east to keep an eye on the French. Wellington's army was thus deployed on a north–south line, about 12 km long, between the Dos Casas and Turon rivers. About 10 km west of Fort Concepcion was the fortress of Almeida, held by a French garrison now blockaded by Wellington's troops.

Masséna Moves West

With the Anglo-Portuguese army spread between Aldea del Obispo and Fuentes de Oñoro, Masséna saw an opportunity to strike. On 2 May, he led his army out of Ciudad Rodrigo. The objective was the relief of Almeida and the defeat of Wellington's army, which stood between him and the fortress. This was a tall order by any standard, but Masséna knew this was his last chance to restore his tarnished reputation by striking a victorious blow. It would instantly vindicate him in the eyes of Napoleon and of his own army. Almeida, the key to Portugal, would be secured and the route opened for another invasion.

A French view of the battle of Fuentes de Oñoro on 5 May 1811 after Martinet. The foreground shows an attack by the French dragoons on infantry in the first phase of the battle. There are of course no mountains in the area such as shown in the background.

The men who marched out of Ciudad Rodrigo were motivated by the prospect of striking at the Anglo-Portuguese and relieving their comrades holding Almeida. After all the humiliations and the retreat from Portugal, the opportunity to attack the hated 'Anglais' was welcome. All knew that Masséna had once been a great general and that, with a bit of luck, he could lead them to victory.

The French army marched west on two parallel roads. Predictably, the Allied forward piquets spotted them and there was much skirmishing between the French and Allied scouts. The Light Division gradually fell back before the advancing French troops, who became visible to Wellington's Allied army as they marched forward during the afternoon. Three columns of troops with about 2–3 km between each could be seen on the plain east of the Dos Casas River. The 2nd Corps formed the northern column marching on the road leading to Aldea do Obispo and ultimately to Fortress Almeida. Next came the centre column made up of the 8th Corps which had only one division marching in the general direction of Sao Pedro. The column to the south was the most powerful with the entire 6th Corps followed by the 9th Corps, which was not yet visible. This column numbering over 30,000 men, was heading straight for the village of Fuentes de Oñoro.

Masséna had concentrated the majority of his forces in a strong southern column, as he suspected that Fuentes de Oñoro was the key to the Anglo-Portuguese position. During the afternoon of 2 May he rode with his staff officers to survey Wellington's positions. This convinced him that Fuentes de Oñoro was the place to attack. If it fell, not only would part of Wellington's army be lost, but his line could be rolled up

ANGLO-PORTUGUESE

1 Light companies from 2/24th, 2/42nd, 1/79th, 1/50th, 1/71st, 1/92nd, 1st, 2nd, 5th and 7th line battalions of the King's German Legion, 1/45th, 74th, 1/88th, 2/83rd, 2/88th, 94th, 9th and 21st Portuguese infantry; two extra light companies from the King's German Legion; four rifle companies from the 5/60th and one company from the 3/95th Rifles. Commanded by LtCol Williams, 5/60th Foot. An additional 460 men of 2/83rd Foot were also in the village of Fuentes de Oñoro.

2 1st Division (Lieutenant-General Spencer)
1st Brigade (Colonel Stopford)
1/2nd Coldstream Guards, 1/3rd Scots Guards, 5/60th Foot (Rifles) - 1 coy
2nd Brigade (Major-General Nightingale)
2/24th, 2 /42nd, 1/79th, 5/60th Foot [Rifles] - 1 coy
3rd Brigade (Major-General Howard)
1/50th, 1/71st, 1/92nd, 3/95th Rifles - 1 coy
4th Brigade (Major-General von Löwe)
1st, 2nd, 5th & 7th Line Bns. King's German Legion
Light Bn. KGL - 2 coys

3 3rd Division (Major-General Picton)
1st Brigade (Colonel Mackinnon)
74th, 1/88th, 1/45th Foot, 5/60th Foot (Rifles) - 3 coys
2nd Brigade (Major-General Colville)
2/5th, 2/83rd, 2/88th, 94th
3rd Brigade (Colonel Power)
9th & 21st Portuguese Infantry

4 7th Division (Major-General Houston)
1st Brigade (Major-General Sontag):
2/51st, 85th, Chasseurs Britanniques, Brunswick-Oels - 8 coys
2nd Brigade (Brigadier-General Doyle):
7th & 19th Portuguese Infantry
2nd Cazadores

5 Light Division (Brigadier-General Craufurd)
1st Brigade (Lieutenant-Colonel Beckwith)
1/43rd foot, 1/95th Rifles - 4 coys, 2/95th Rifles - 1 coy, 3rd Cazadores
2nd Brigade (Colonel Drummond)
1/52nd, 2/52nd Foot, 1/95th Rifles - 4 coys, 1st Cazadores

6 1st Cavalry Brigade (Major-General Slade)
1st Dragoons, 14th Light Dragoons

7 2nd Cavalry Brigade (Lieutenant-Colonel von Arentschild)
16th Light Dragoons, 1st Hussars, KGL

8 6th Division (Major-General Campbell)
1st Brigade (Colonel Hulse)
1/11th, 2/53rd, 1/61st, 5/60th Foot (Rifles) - 1 coy
2nd Brigade (Colonel Burne)
1/36th, 2nd Foot
3rd Brigade (Colonel Madden)
8th & 12th Portuguese Infantry

9 5th Division (Major-General Erskine)
1st Brigade (Brigadier-General Hay)
3/1st, 1/9th, 2/38th Foot, Brunswick-Oels - 1 coy
2nd Brigade (Major-General Dunlop)
1/4th, 2/30th, 3/44th, Brunswick-Oels - 1 coy
3rd Brigade (Brigadier-General Spry)
3rd & 15th Portuguese Infantry
8th Cazadores

10 3rd Brigade (Brigadier-General de Barbacena) - Guarding the Allied northern flank
4th & 10th Portuguese Cavalry

11 British detachment posted at Pozo Bello guarding the Allied southern flank.

12 Sir Denis Pack's Independent Portuguese Brigade

13 Don Julian Sanchez's Spanish guerrilla cavalry.

FRENCH

A 6th Corps (Major-General Loison)
1st Division: Marchand
Brigade Maucune
1, 2 & 4/6th Light Infantry
1, 2 & 4/69th Line Infantry
Brigade Chemineau
1, 2 & 3/39th Line Infantry
1, 2 & 3/76th Line Infantry
2nd Division: Mermet
Brigade Ménard
1, 2 & 4/25th Light Infantry
1, 2 & 4/27th Line Infantry
Brigade Taupin
1, 2 & 4/50th Line Infantry
1, 2 & 4/59th Line Infantry
3rd Division: Ferey
4, 5 & 6/26th Line Infantry
Légion du Midi - 1 bn.
Légion Hanovrienne - 1 bn.
4, 5 & 6/66th Line Infantry
4 & 6/82nd Line Infantry

B 9th Corps (General of Division Drouet, Count d'Erlon)
Division: Claparède
54th Line Infantry - 1bn.
21st Light Infantry - 1bn.
28th Light Infantry - 1bn.
40th Line Infantry - 1bn.
63rd Line Infantry - 1bn.
88th Line Infantry - 1bn.

64th Line Infantry - 1bn.
100th Line Infantry - 1bn.
103rd Line Infantry - 1bn.
Division: Conroux
16th Light Infantry - 1bn.
9th Light Infantry - 1bn.
27th Light Infantry - 1bn.
8th Line Infantry - 1bn.
24th Line Infantry - 1bn.
45th Line Infantry - 1bn.
94th Line Infantry - 1bn.
95th Line Infantry - 1bn.
96th Line Infantry - 1bn.

C *Cavalry Brigade Lamotte (from Loison's 6th Corps)*
3rd Hussars, 15th Chasseurs à cheval

D 8th Corps (General Junot, Duke of Abrantes)
2nd Division: Solignac
1, 2 & 3/15th Line Infantry
1, 2 & 3/86th Line Infantry
1, 2 & 4/65th Line Infantry
Régiment Irlandais (Irish Regiment) - 1 bn

E 2nd Corps (General Reynier)
2nd Division Heudelet
Brigade Godard
1, 2 &3/17th Light Infantry

1, 2 & 3/70th Line Infantry
Brigade Arnaud
1, 2 & 3/31st Light Infantry
1, 2 & 3/47th Line Infantry

F 2nd Corps (General Reynier)
1st Division: Merle
Brigade Sarrut
1, 2 & 3/2nd Light Infantry
1, 2 & 3/36th Line Infantry
Brigade Graindorge
1, 2 & 3/4th Light Infantry

G 2nd Corps (General Reynier)
Cavalry Brigade
1st Hussars, 22nd Chasseurs à cheval, 8th Dragons

H Montbrun's and Fournier's Cavalry
Reserve of Cavalry: General Montbrun
Brigade Cavrois:
3rd, 6th & 15th Dragoons
Brigade Ornano
6th, 11th & 25th Dragoons
Brigade Fournier (from Drouet's 9th Corps):
7th, 13th & 20th Chasseurs à cheval

I French garrison of Almeida

XXXX
Anglo-Portugese
WELLINGTON

13. PHASE 4 Wellington sends 1/71st, 1/79th and 2/24th from Spencer's 1st Division. Led by Colonel Cadogan, they charge into the village and halt the French.

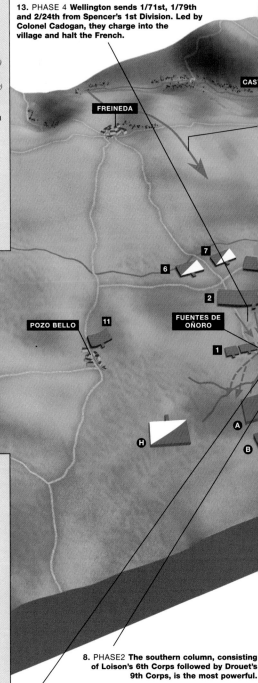

CAS

FREINEDA

7

6

2

FUENTES DE OÑORO

POZO BELLO   11

1

13

NAVE DE AVER

A

H

B

8. PHASE2 The southern column, consisting of Loison's 6th Corps followed by Drouet's 9th Corps, is the most powerful.

12. PHASE 4 Early afternoon, 3 May, six French infantry battalions of the 1st Brigade, Ferey's Division attacks Fuentes de Oñoro. Waiting for them in the village are 1,800 elite light infantry and 460 men the 2/83rd Foot. The 4,200 French start to overwhelm the 2,200 Allied troops.

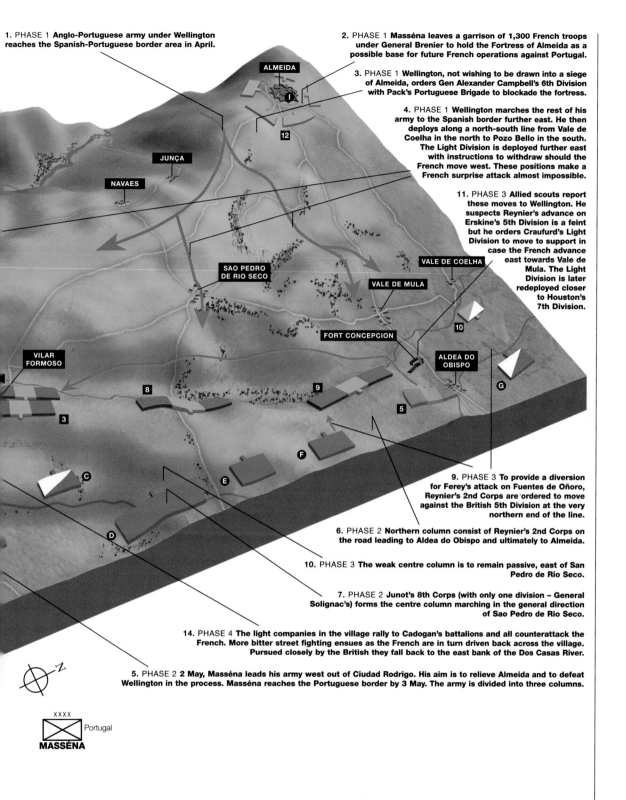

1. PHASE 1 **Anglo-Portuguese army under Wellington reaches the Spanish-Portuguese border area in April.**

2. PHASE 1 **Masséna leaves a garrison of 1,300 French troops under General Brenier to hold the Fortress of Almeida as a possible base for future French operations against Portugal.**

3. PHASE 1 **Wellington, not wishing to be drawn into a siege of Almeida, orders Gen Alexander Campbell's 6th Division with Pack's Portuguese Brigade to blockade the fortress.**

4. PHASE 1 **Wellington marches the rest of his army to the Spanish border further east. He then deploys along a north-south line from Vale de Coelha in the north to Pozo Bello in the south. The Light Division is deployed further east with instructions to withdraw should the French move west. These positions make a French surprise attack almost impossible.**

11. PHASE 3 **Allied scouts report these moves to Wellington. He suspects Reynier's advance on Erskine's 5th Division is a feint but he orders Craufurd's Light Division to move to support in case the French advance east towards Vale de Mula. The Light Division is later redeployed closer to Houston's 7th Division.**

9. PHASE 3 **To provide a diversion for Ferey's attack on Fuentes de Oñoro, Reynier's 2nd Corps are ordered to move against the British 5th Division at the very northern end of the line.**

6. PHASE 2 **Northern column consist of Reynier's 2nd Corps on the road leading to Aldea do Obispo and ultimately to Almeida.**

10. PHASE 3 **The weak centre column is to remain passive, east of San Pedro de Rio Seco.**

7. PHASE 2 **Junot's 8th Corps (with only one division – General Solignac's) forms the centre column marching in the general direction of Sao Pedro de Rio Seco.**

14. PHASE 4 **The light companies in the village rally to Cadogan's battalions and all counterattack the French. More bitter street fighting ensues as the French are in turn driven back across the village. Pursued closely by the British they fall back to the east bank of the Dos Casas River.**

5. PHASE 2 **2 May, Masséna leads his army west out of Ciudad Rodrigo. His aim is to relieve Almeida and to defeat Wellington in the process. Masséna reaches the Portuguese border by 3 May. The army is divided into three columns.**

Map labels: ALMEIDA, JUNÇA, NAVAES, SAO PEDRO DE RIO SECO, VALE DE COELHA, VALE DE MULA, FORT CONCEPCION, ALDEA DO OBISPO, VILAR FORMOSO

XXXX
Portugal
MASSÉNA

THE ATTACK OF FEREY'S DIVISION

Fuentes de Oñoro, Afternoon, 3 May 1811. Viewed from the south-east showing the initial French attempt to storm the village two days before the main battle.

from the south. With luck, the majority of the British and Portuguese soldiers would not escape, the Allied army would be destroyed and Wellington killed or disgraced.

Wellington had just as shrewd a battlefield eye as Masséna, and he also recognised the importance of Fuentes de Oñoro. The Allied troops in Fuentes de Oñoro's immediate vicinity numbered some 24,000 men, most of them – in typical Wellington style – concealed from the French on the high ground behind the village.

The fields southwest of Fuentes de Oñoro. This is the area that Masséna hoped his cavalry would sweep across and outflank the Allied army on the morning of 5 May 1811. It proved to be well protected by Wellington's second defence line. (Photo: RC)

THE ACTION OF 3 MAY

Ferey's Division from Loison's 6th Corps was ordered by Masséna to storm Fuentes de Oñoro. It had ten battalions numbering 4,200 men for the task. As a diversion, the northern column (Reynier's 2nd Corps) was ordered to launch a feint against the British 5th Division at the very northern end of the line. The weak centre column would remain east of San Pedro. All these movements were reported to Wellington by Allied scouts. He naturally suspected that the northern column's moves towards the 5th Division were merely probes intended to fool him, but he ordered Craufurd's Light Division to move up closer should the French close in.

In the early afternoon, the six French infantry battalions of the first brigade of Ferey's Division attacked Fuentes de Oñoro. Waiting for them were 1,800 elite troops under the command of Lieutenant-Colonel W. Williams of the 5/60th consisting of the light companies drawn from 17 British and four Portuguese battalions, two extra light companies from the King's German Legion, four rifle companies from the 5/60th and one company from the 3/95th Rifles. An additional 460 men belonging to the 2/83rd Foot were also in the village.[20]

As soon as the French battalions came within range to the east the Allies opened fire, but with little effect, and the French pressed on. The shallow Dos Casas River was practically dry, and they crossed it easily and took possession of some houses on the lower slope next to the river. The

Field west of Fuentes de Oñoro on a plateau just past the village. This area was where Picton's 3rd Brigade was posted in reserve, ready to reinforce troops defending the village. (Photo: RC)

Allies counter-charged and the French started to withdraw. General Ferey was on the spot and ordered the five battalions of his second brigade to attack. Desperate fighting ensued in the narrow streets and houses of the village. According to Marbot, the attack of the second brigade might have succeeded but for a case of 'friendly fire' in the confusion of battle; in their red tunics the French Hanoverian Legion were mistaken for British infantry and fired upon by the French 66th Line Infantry. Despite the confusion caused by this error, the French slowly forced the British and Portuguese to withdraw through the village. The Allied light companies fought stubbornly into the late afternoon at the foot of the hill behind the village and near Fuentes de Oñoro's little church.

Wellington was watching all this from the hill further back. By now the 4,200 French were overwhelming his 2,200 Allied troops and it was time to commit more British troops. The 1/71st, 1/79th and 2/24th were called up from Spencer's 1st Division. Led by Colonel Henry Cadogan, the three battalions charged into the village and stopped the French. 'How different the duty of a French officer to ours', recalled a soldier of the 71st who was there. 'They stimulating their men by their example, the vociferating, each chaffing each other as they appear in a fury, shouting, to the points of our bayonets' while 'after the first huzza the British officers, restraining their men, still as death' and 'Steady, lads, steady, is all you hear, and that in an undertone.' William's light companies rallied alongside Cadogan's men and together they counter-attacked the French. More bitter lane-to-lane and house-to-house fighting ensued now as the French in their turn fell back through the village and then across to the east bank of the Dos Casas River. They were followed closely by the British. The men of the 1/71st even crossed the river and advanced up its eastern slope, but they were now too far ahead to be supported and retreated back to the western bank. All the ground gained by the French during the afternoon had been lost.

Marshal Masséna, watching the fighting from a distance, now called up four battalions from Marchand's division to cover Ferey's retreating men and allow them to rally. The four French battalions, and other troops that had quickly rallied, secured the ground as far as the east bank of the Dos Casas River. The west bank was held by Wellington's men and the French

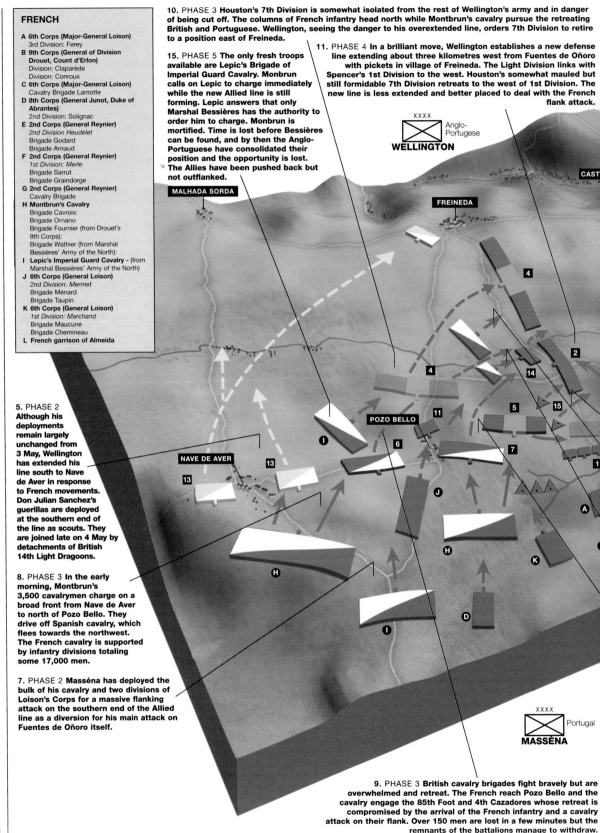

FRENCH

A **6th Corps (Major-General Loison)**
 3rd Division: Ferey
B **9th Corps (General of Division Drouet, Count d'Erlon)**
 Division: Claparède
 Division: Conroux
C **6th Corps (Major-General Loison)**
 Cavalry Brigade Lamotte
D **8th Corps (General Junot, Duke of Abrantes)**
 2nd Division: Solignac
E **2nd Corps (General Reynier)**
 2nd Division Heudelet
 Brigade Godard
 Brigade Arnaud
F **2nd Corps (General Reynier)**
 1st Division: Merle
 Brigade Sarrut
 Brigade Graindorge
G **2nd Corps (General Reynier)**
 Cavalry Brigade
H **Montbrun's Cavalry**
 Brigade Cavrois:
 Brigade Ornano
 Brigade Fournier (from Drouet's 9th Corps):
 Brigade Wathier (from Marshal Bessières' Army of the North):
I **Lepic's Imperial Guard Cavalry** - (from Marshal Bessières' Army of the North)
J **6th Corps (General Loison)**
 2nd Division: Mermet
 Brigade Ménard
 Brigade Taupin
K **6th Corps (General Loison)**
 1st Division: Marchand
 Brigade Maucune
 Brigade Chemineau
L **French garrison of Almeida**

10. PHASE 3 Houston's 7th Division is somewhat isolated from the rest of Wellington's army and in danger of being cut off. The columns of French infantry head north while Montbrun's cavalry pursue the retreating British and Portuguese. Wellington, seeing the danger to his overextended line, orders 7th Division to retire to a position east of Freineda.

15. PHASE 5 The only fresh troops available are Lepic's Brigade of Imperial Guard Cavalry. Monbrun calls on Lepic to charge immediately while the new Allied line is still forming. Lepic answers that only Marshal Bessières has the authority to order him to charge. Monbrun is mortified. Time is lost before Bessières can be found, and by then the Anglo-Portuguese have consolidated their position and the opportunity is lost. The Allies have been pushed back but not outflanked.

MALHADA SORDA

11. PHASE 4 In a brilliant move, Wellington establishes a new defense line extending about three kilometres west from Fuentes de Oñoro with pickets in village of Freineda. The Light Division links with Spencer's 1st Division to the west. Houston's somewhat mauled but still formidable 7th Division retreats to the west of 1st Division. The new line is less extended and better placed to deal with the French flank attack.

xxxx
Anglo-Portugese
WELLINGTON

CAST

FREINEDA

5. PHASE 2 Although his deployments remain largely unchanged from 3 May, Wellington has extended his line south to Nave de Aver in response to French movements. Don Julian Sanchez's guerillas are deployed at the southern end of the line as scouts. They are joined late on 4 May by detachments of British 14th Light Dragoons.

NAVE DE AVER

POZO BELLO

8. PHASE 3 In the early morning, Montbrun's 3,500 cavalrymen charge on a broad front from Nave de Aver to north of Pozo Bello. They drive off Spanish cavalry, which flees towards the northwest. The French cavalry is supported by infantry divisions totaling some 17,000 men.

7. PHASE 2 Masséna has deployed the bulk of his cavalry and two divisions of Loison's Corps for a massive flanking attack on the southern end of the Allied line as a diversion for his main attack on Fuentes de Oñoro itself.

xxxx
Portugal
MASSÉNA

9. PHASE 3 British cavalry brigades fight bravely but are overwhelmed and retreat. The French reach Pozo Bello and the cavalry engage the 85th Foot and 4th Cazadores whose retreat is compromised by the arrival of the French infantry and a cavalry attack on their flank. Over 150 men are lost in a few minutes but the remnants of the battalions manage to withdraw.

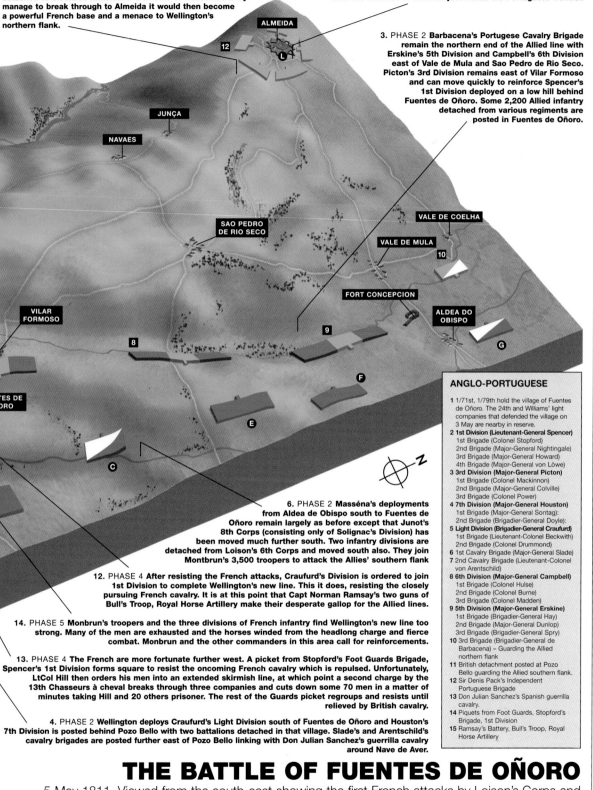

2. PHASE 1 **Pack's Independent Portuguese Brigade has been detached to blockade Almeida. If elements of Masséna's army manage to break through to Almeida it would then become a powerful French base and a menace to Wellington's northern flank.**

1. PHASE 1 **French garrison of 1,300 troops under General Brenier hold the Fortress of Almeida just inside the Portuguese frontier.**

3. PHASE 2 **Barbacena's Portuguese Cavalry Brigade remain the northern end of the Allied line with Erskine's 5th Division and Campbell's 6th Division east of Vale de Mula and Sao Pedro de Rio Seco. Picton's 3rd Division remains east of Vilar Formoso and can move quickly to reinforce Spencer's 1st Division deployed on a low hill behind Fuentes de Oñoro. Some 2,200 Allied infantry detached from various regiments are posted in Fuentes de Oñoro.**

ALMEIDA

12

JUNÇA

NAVAES

SAO PEDRO DE RIO SECO

VALE DE COELHA

VALE DE MULA

10

FORT CONCEPCION

VILAR FORMOSO

ALDEA DO OBISPO

8

9

G

F

E

C

TES DE ORO

6. PHASE 2 **Masséna's deployments from Aldea de Obispo south to Fuentes de Oñoro remain largely as before except that Junot's 8th Corps (consisting only of Solignac's Division) has been moved much further south. Two infantry divisions are detached from Loison's 6th Corps and moved south also. They join Montbrun's 3,500 troopers to attack the Allies' southern flank.**

12. PHASE 4 **After resisting the French attacks, Craufurd's Division is ordered to join 1st Division to complete Wellington's new line. This it does, resisting the closely pursuing French cavalry. It is at this point that Capt Norman Ramsay's two guns of Bull's Troop, Royal Horse Artillery make their desperate gallop for the Allied lines.**

14. PHASE 5 **Monbrun's troopers and the three divisions of French infantry find Wellington's new line too strong. Many of the men are exhausted and the horses winded from the headlong charge and fierce combat. Monbrun and the other commanders in this area call for reinforcements.**

13. PHASE 4 **The French are more fortunate further west. A picket from Stopford's Foot Guards Brigade, Spencer's 1st Division forms square to resist the oncoming French cavalry which is repulsed. Unfortunately, LtCol Hill then orders his men into an extended skirmish line, at which point a second charge by the 13th Chasseurs à cheval breaks through three companies and cuts down some 70 men in a matter of minutes taking Hill and 20 others prisoner. The rest of the Guards picket regroups and resists until relieved by British cavalry.**

4. PHASE 2 **Wellington deploys Craufurd's Light Division south of Fuentes de Oñoro and Houston's 7th Division is posted behind Pozo Bello with two battalions detached in that village. Slade's and Arentschild's cavalry brigades are posted further east of Pozo Bello linking with Don Julian Sanchez's guerrilla cavalry around Nave de Aver.**

ANGLO-PORTUGUESE

1 **1/71st, 1/79th hold the village of Fuentes de Oñoro. The 24th and Williams' light companies that defended the village on 3 May are nearby in reserve.**
2 **1st Division (Lieutenant-General Spencer)**
 1st Brigade (Colonel Stopford)
 2nd Brigade (Major-General Nightingale)
 3rd Brigade (Major-General Howard)
 4th Brigade (Major-General von Löwe)
3 **3rd Division (Major-General Picton)**
 1st Brigade (Colonel Mackinnon)
 2nd Brigade (Major-General Colville)
 3rd Brigade (Colonel Power)
4 **7th Division (Major-General Houston)**
 1st Brigade (Major-General Sontag):
 2nd Brigade (Brigadier-General Doyle):
5 **Light Division (Brigadier-General Craufurd)**
 1st Brigade (Lieutenant-Colonel Beckwith)
 2nd Brigade (Colonel Drummond)
6 **1st Cavalry Brigade (Major-General Slade)**
7 **2nd Cavalry Brigade (Lieutenant-Colonel von Arentschild)**
8 **6th Division (Major-General Campbell)**
 1st Brigade (Colonel Hulse)
 2nd Brigade (Colonel Burne)
 3rd Brigade (Colonel Madden)
9 **5th Division (Major-General Erskine)**
 1st Brigade (Brigadier-General Hay)
 2nd Brigade (Major-General Dunlop)
 3rd Brigade (Brigadier-General Spry)
10 **3rd Brigade (Brigadier-General de Barbacena) – Guarding the Allied northern flank**
11 **British detachment posted at Pozo Bello guarding the Allied southern flank.**
12 **Sir Denis Pack's Independent Portuguese Brigade**
13 **Don Julian Sanchez's Spanish guerrilla cavalry.**
14 **Piquets from Foot Guards, Stopford's Brigade, 1st Division**
15 **Ramsay's Battery, Bull's Troop, Royal Horse Artillery**

THE BATTLE OF FUENTES DE OÑORO
5 May 1811. Viewed from the south-east showing the first French attacks by Loison's Corps and Montbrun's cavalry and the Allied retreat to Wellington's second defensive line.

The small church of Fuentes de Oñoro as seen from the west. It was the scene of heavy fighting on 5 May 1811. The bayonet charge by the 88th Foot hit the French at this spot. (Photo: RC)

did not mount another attack. The shooting died down as night came and both sides remained in their positions.

Once again, a French assault against Wellington's positions had failed with heavy casualties. Ferey's Division suffered 652 men, killed, wounded or taken prisoner; this figure included three officers and 164 men captured when the troops led by Cadogan had recaptured the village. By comparison, the Allied losses were much lower at 259 killed or wounded including 48 Portuguese.

This initial engagement had showed Masséna that the Allied forces were well dug in at Fuentes de Oñoro. The frontal assault had failed but it remained to be seen if the village could be outflanked. Masséna had previously outflanked Wellington successfully after the battle of Bussaco. Cavalry General Montbrun dispatched reconnaissance parties in every direction to make a thorough survey of the Anglo-Portuguese positions.

From early in the morning of 4 May, parties of French cavalry could be seen riding back and forth at various points north and south of Fuentes de Oñoro. In the village itself, British troops were dug in, taking cover behind stone walls and houses. French troops just across the Dos Casas River had done the same. The enemies were close to each other, separated only by the practically dried-out riverbed, each expecting the other to attack. During the morning, intense firing broke out and continued until sometime before noon, when it finally died away. It seems the French thought the British would try to drive them out of the houses near the river. However, the British had no such plans.

In the afternoon, cavalrymen began returning with their reconnaissance reports. From these, General Montbrun now gained a much better idea of Wellington's positions, which he reported to Masséna. The Allied army's positions north of Fuentes de Oñoro were strong and there was no realistic chance of a breakthrough in that area. Reports coming in from the south and southwest revealed that the villages of Pozo Bello and Nava de Aver had nothing but a line of cavalry piquets in front of them and a battalion of infantry in Pozo Bello. From these reports, Masséna determined the next move.

THE MAIN BATTLE OF 5 MAY

The obvious place to concentrate an attack to outflank the Allied army was to the south of Fuentes de Oñoro. For the attack to succeed the pressure would have to be maintained on the village and points further north so that Wellington could not detach troops to the south to resist the French flanking movement.

Three infantry divisions totalling 17,000 men were assigned to carry out the flanking movement: Marchand's and Mermet's divisions from the 6th Corps and Solignac's from the 8th Corps. The cavalry would consist of Montbrun's dragoon division and the three brigades under Fournier, Lepic and Wathier for a total of 3,500 troopers. The total attack force, all fresh troops, would thus be 20,500-men strong. These troops would move south of Fuentes de Oñoro and then west at Pozo Bello and its vicinity heading towards Freneda.

To keep the pressure on the rest of Wellington's line, some 14,000 men in three divisions would attack the village of Fuentes de Oñoro. Further north, Reynier's Corps would make limited attacks on the Allied line. If it proved weakly defended, a major attack would be launched.

This was a complex but sound plan, certainly better than any of Masséna's previous battle plans since entering Portugal in 1810. He knew he had a definite numerical advantage over Wellington although probably not the extent of it. Masséna in fact outnumbered Wellington by some 11,000 men. As darkness fell on 4 May, Masséna's 48,500 men started moving to their appointed position for the attack the next morning.

While Masséna was planning, Allied army scouts were watching every French movement. Wellington considered good intelligence of the utmost importance and his headquarters was alive with cavalry and staff officers riding in and out with the latest information. His Portuguese Corps of Mounted Guides was attached to his immediate staff and included officers and troopers that were familiar with the country and who could generally assess the quality of information from prisoners and deserters. Communication with distant Lisbon could be remarkably swift thanks to the newly created Portuguese army telegraph corps. Now that the Allied army was entering Spain, the guerrillas of Don Julian Sanchez eagerly provided Wellington with intelligence on the movements of the French.

The French had nothing like the intelligence network that had been developed by the British and Portuguese. One of Masséna's staff officers, Pelet, later wrote that 'the bands of Spanish insurgents and the English army supported each other. Without the English the Spanish would have been quickly dispersed or crushed. In the absence of the guerrillas, the French armies would have acquired a unity and strength that they were never able to achieve in this country, and the Anglo-Portuguese army, unwarned of our operations and projects, would have been unable to withstand concentrated operations.'

From Wellington's perspective, the intelligence being received on 4 May spoke of a remarkably quiet French army. As he 'never slept comfortably' when opposed by Masséna, Wellington was sure something was afoot. Clearly another attack … but where? His flanks seemed the most likely target. The northern flank seemed secure so it had to be the southern flank, which was indeed where most of the French army was poised. Late in the day, his scouts noticed stirrings in the French camps. They were preparing to move. Wellington ordered his four British regiments of cavalry to string out to the south with mounted guerrillas of Don Julian Sanchez at the far southern end near Nava de Aver. Stretched over 5 km, it was not a strong formation and would not stop an enemy

OVERLEAF
Masséna noted that Wellington's southern flank was overextended and ordered the bulk of his cavalry to assault the Allied right supported by three infantry divisions. Thousands of French troopers swept through the village of Pozo Bello defended by the British 85th Foot and 2nd Portuguese Cazadores. The defenders were badly mauled in the ensuing melee but, like most of the troops on Wellington's right, managed to retreat to the strong new defense line established further north. (Patrice Courcelle)

force, but it would provide a first obstacle. The 4,500 men of Houston's 7th Division were ordered to move south and post themselves behind the village of Pozo Bello, except for the 85th Foot and the 2nd Cazadores stationed in the village itself.

The Spanish guerrillas of Don Julian Sanchez had had lookouts at Nava de Aver since 3 May. On the evening of the 4th, they were joined by two squadrons of the 14th Light Dragoons. At daybreak on 5 May Major T.W. Brotherton asked Don Julian to show him where he had posted his forward piquets. Don Julian saw horsemen in the fog to the east and thought they were his lookouts. Brotherton was dubious as it seemed like a lot of horsemen for a piquet. As the fog lifted, Brotherton recalled, they were seen to be 'a whole French regiment dismounted. They now mounted immediately and advanced against us.'

Captain Ramsay and his Royal Horse Artillery gunners galloping through the French in his famous and successful bid to save his two guns at the battle of Fuentes de Oñoro in the morning of 5 May 1811.

THE FRENCH CAVALRY CHARGES

It was the first wave of Monbrun's dragoons followed by a mass of troopers who seemed to cover the plain to the east. The Spanish guerrillas were surprised by the French dragoons and galloped off to the west without offering resistance. Hordes of French dragoons now galloped past Nava de Aver. The two squadrons of the British 14th Light Dragoons retreated to the northwest, fighting off the French troopers as they fell back. At this point, the main body of French cavalry encountered the British 16th Light Dragoons and the 1st Hussars of the King's German Legion, who were posted further north, forming a line between Nava de Aver and Pozo Bello. The 16th and the hussars formed up and, rather amazingly, charged the French cavalry in an attempt to halt them. They lost many men, soon realised they would be overwhelmed and galloped back to Pozo Bello pursued by hordes of French troopers. Brotherton's two squadrons of the 14th Light Dragoons, who were also retreating from further south, now arrived at Pozo Bello.

By then, masses of French dragoons were closing in on the village of Pozo Bello. It was about 7.00am and, up until now, only French cavalry had been engaged. Infantry arrived on the scene in the form of the two divisions of Generals Marchand and Mermet. Marchand's Division, some 12 battalions totalling nearly 5,900 men, moved up to Pozo Bello. The French voltigeurs rapidly cleared the woods just east of the village of its Anglo-Portuguese skirmishers and then charged into the hamlet. The 85th Foot and the 2nd Cazadores knew they could not stand for long against such odds and retreated north from the village, but it was already

Captain Ramsay saving his guns at Fuentes de Oñoro according to a print in Stoqueller's 1852 biography of Wellington.

Captain Ramsay saving his guns at Fuentes de Oñoro according to a print after Harry Payne.

almost too late. As the British and Portuguese soldiers streamed out of Pozo Bello, they were unexpectedly set upon by a large body of French cavalry on their flank. Within a few minutes, the 85th and 2nd Cazadores lost 150 men but the rest of the battalions managed to get away thanks to two squadrons of the King's German Legion hussars who charged the oncoming French. A few companies of the 95th Rifles also came to the rescue, and Costello recalled seeing that 'the 85th Regiment, in their conspicuous red dresses, were being very roughly handled by the enemy in this, their first engagement since arriving in the country.' This assistance allowed the two Allied battalions time to form a new defence line running westward and linking with the 7th Division 2 km away.

The 7th Division was rather isolated from the rest of Wellington's army and there was a real possibility that it might be cut off. The battalions of French infantry coming out of Pozo Bello were formed into columns heading north while Montbrun's cavalry were in pursuit of the retreating British and Portuguese. Wellington could see all this and realised the danger to the 7th Division. It was equally clear that Masséna and his generals had also seen the weakness of his overextended line to the south. Wellington ordered that a new defence line be established running west from Fuentes de Oñoro for about 3 km with piquets as far as the village of Freneda. The Light Division formed a line from Fuentes de Oñoro with Spencer's 1st Division west of it. Houston's somewhat mauled but still formidable

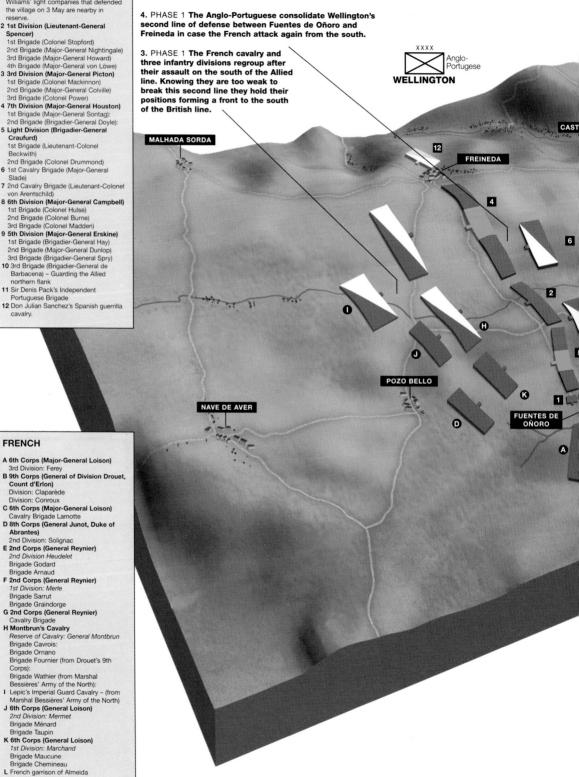

ANGLO-PORTUGUESE

1 1/71st, 1/79th hold the village of Fuentes de Oñoro. The 24th and Williams' light companies that defended the village on 3 May are nearby in reserve.
2 1st Division (Lieutenant-General Spencer)
  1st Brigade (Colonel Stopford)
  2nd Brigade (Major-General Nightingale)
  3rd Brigade (Major-General Howard)
  4th Brigade (Major-General von Löwe)
3 3rd Division (Major-General Picton)
  1st Brigade (Colonel Mackinnon)
  2nd Brigade (Major-General Colville)
  3rd Brigade (Colonel Power)
4 7th Division (Major-General Houston)
  1st Brigade (Major-General Sontag):
  2nd Brigade (Brigadier-General Doyle):
5 Light Division (Brigadier-General Craufurd)
  1st Brigade (Lieutenant-Colonel Beckwith)
  2nd Brigade (Colonel Drummond)
6 1st Cavalry Brigade (Major-General Slade)
7 2nd Cavalry Brigade (Lieutenant-Colonel von Arentschild)
8 6th Division (Major-General Campbell)
  1st Brigade (Colonel Hulse)
  2nd Brigade (Colonel Burne)
  3rd Brigade (Colonel Madden)
9 5th Division (Major-General Erskine)
  1st Brigade (Brigadier-General Hay)
  2nd Brigade (Major-General Dunlop)
  3rd Brigade (Brigadier-General Spry)
10 3rd Brigade (Brigadier-General de Barbacena) – Guarding the Allied northern flank
11 Sir Denis Pack's Independent Portuguese Brigade
12 Don Julian Sanchez's Spanish guerrilla cavalry.

FRENCH

A 6th Corps (Major-General Loison)
  3rd Division: Ferey
B 9th Corps (General of Division Drouet, Count d'Erlon)
  Division: Claparède
  Division: Conroux
C 6th Corps (Major-General Loison)
  Cavalry Brigade Lamotte
D 8th Corps (General Junot, Duke of Abrantes)
  2nd Division: Solignac
E 2nd Corps (General Reynier)
  2nd Division Heudelet
  Brigade Godard
  Brigade Arnaud
F 2nd Corps (General Reynier)
  1st Division: Merle
  Brigade Sarrut
  Brigade Graindorge
G 2nd Corps (General Reynier)
  Cavalry Brigade
H Montbrun's Cavalry
  Reserve of Cavalry: General Montbrun
  Brigade Cavrois:
  Brigade Ornano
  Brigade Fournier (from Drouet's 9th Corps):
  Brigade Wathier (from Marshal Bessières' Army of the North)
I Lepic's Imperial Guard Cavalry – (from Marshal Bessières' Army of the North)
J 6th Corps (General Loison)
  2nd Division: Mermet
  Brigade Ménard
  Brigade Taupin
K 6th Corps (General Loison)
  1st Division: Marchand
  Brigade Maucune
  Brigade Chemineau
L French garrison of Almeida

4. PHASE 1 The Anglo-Portuguese consolidate Wellington's second line of defense between Fuentes de Oñoro and Freineda in case the French attack again from the south.

3. PHASE 1 The French cavalry and three infantry divisions regroup after their assault on the south of the Allied line. Knowing they are too weak to break this second line they hold their positions forming a front to the south of the British line.

XXXX
Anglo-Portuguese
WELLINGTON

MALHADA SORDA

CAST

12

FREINEDA

4

6

2

I

H

J

K

1

POZO BELLO

NAVE DE AVER

D

FUENTES DE OÑORO

A

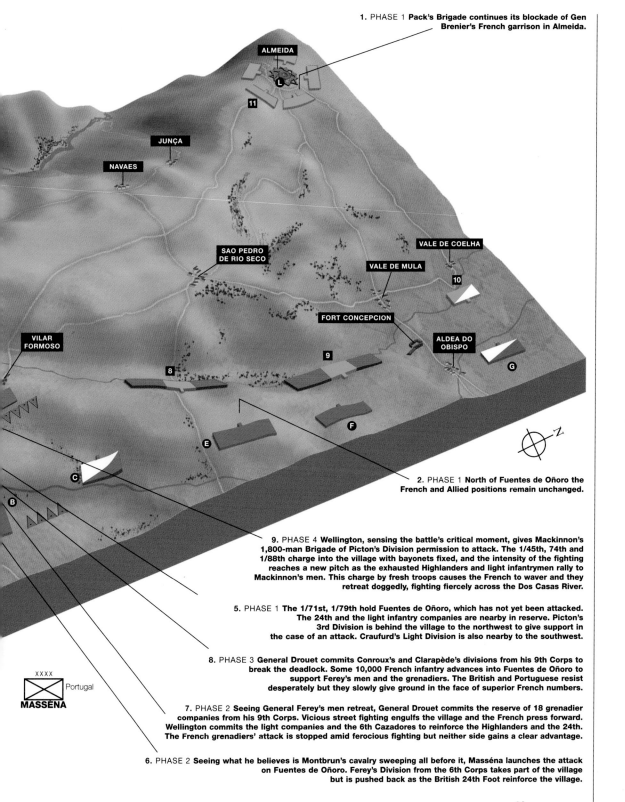

1. PHASE 1 **Pack's Brigade continues its blockade of Gen Brenier's French garrison in Almeida.**

ALMEIDA

L

11

JUNÇA

NAVAES

VALE DE COELHA

SAO PEDRO DE RIO SECO

VALE DE MULA

10

FORT CONCEPCION

VILAR FORMOSO

ALDEA DO OBISPO

9

8

G

F

E

C

2. PHASE 1 **North of Fuentes de Oñoro the French and Allied positions remain unchanged.**

B

9. PHASE 4 **Wellington, sensing the battle's critical moment, gives Mackinnon's 1,800-man Brigade of Picton's Division permission to attack. The 1/45th, 74th and 1/88th charge into the village with bayonets fixed, and the intensity of the fighting reaches a new pitch as the exhausted Highlanders and light infantrymen rally to Mackinnon's men. This charge by fresh troops causes the French to waver and they retreat doggedly, fighting fiercely across the Dos Casas River.**

5. PHASE 1 **The 1/71st, 1/79th hold Fuentes de Oñoro, which has not yet been attacked. The 24th and the light infantry companies are nearby in reserve. Picton's 3rd Division is behind the village to the northwest to give support in the case of an attack. Craufurd's Light Division is also nearby to the southwest.**

8. PHASE 3 **General Drouet commits Conroux's and Clarapède's divisions from his 9th Corps to break the deadlock. Some 10,000 French infantry advances into Fuentes de Oñoro to support Ferey's men and the grenadiers. The British and Portuguese resist desperately but they slowly give ground in the face of superior French numbers.**

xxxx

Portugal

MASSÉNA

7. PHASE 2 **Seeing General Ferey's men retreat, General Drouet commits the reserve of 18 grenadier companies from his 9th Corps. Vicious street fighting engulfs the village and the French press forward. Wellington commits the light companies and the 6th Cazadores to reinforce the Highlanders and the 24th. The French grenadiers' attack is stopped amid ferocious fighting but neither side gains a clear advantage.**

6. PHASE 2 **Seeing what he believes is Montbrun's cavalry sweeping all before it, Masséna launches the attack on Fuentes de Oñoro. Ferey's Division from the 6th Corps takes part of the village but is pushed back as the British 24th Foot reinforce the village.**

THE BATTLE OF FUENTES DE OÑORO

5 May 1811. Viewed from the south-east showing the French assault on the village of Fuentes de Oñoro itself.

7th Division would retreat to place itself west of the 1st Division. It was a superb and very rapid tactical move on Wellington's part, testimony to his exceptional ability to react swiftly to unfolding events. This new line was less extended and could still foil the French flanking movement.

Allied Retreat and Ramsay's Feat

Meanwhile, some 2,700 French troopers were sweeping everything before them as they rode north pursuing the 85th Foot and the 2nd Cazadores. To cover the Allied infantrymen and slow down the French, some 1,400 British light cavalry of Slade's and Arentschild's brigades and Bull's Battery of the Royal Horse Artillery stood in the way. Montbrun's dragoons and generals Wathier's and Fournier's brigades of Chasseurs à cheval and hussars clashed with the British 1st Dragoons, the 14th and 16th light dragoons and the King's German Legion's 1st Hussars. It could only be a holding action against the greatly superior French attackers and the British troopers fell back, one squadron fighting while the other retreated before it halted and in turn covered the other squadron's retreat. This fighting lasted for a long time, indicative of the obstinacy of the troopers of both sides. The French believed they had routed the British but, although they lost nearly 160 men, the British troopers remained in formation as they withdrew, eventually falling back past the 7th Division's infantrymen.

During the French cavalry attack that overwhelmed a detachment of the Foot Guards, Captain Home of the 3rd Foot Guards (or Scots Guards) was attacked by three French troopers. A man of uncommon muscular strength, Home repulsed all three. The uniform of the French trooper is erroneous. The 13th Chasseur à cheval did not have helmets nor cuirasses as it was a light cavalry unit wearing shakos and green jackets with orange collar and green cuffs. Brown overalls strapped with leather were often worn in Spain and the men of the 13th still wore queues in 1813. (Print after Harry Payne)

General Houston deployed his 7th Division, which was joined by the 85th Foot and the 2nd Cazadores, at the foot of a gentle slope with some battalions taking cover behind low stone walls. The orderly formation of Montbrun's cavalry was somewhat disrupted as it came face to face with Houston's Division. The French troopers menaced Houston's centre and a French horse artillery battery came up to fire at it while Montbrun sent a brigade of dragoons to outflank the British position on the west side. This seemed to work and they charged towards the British flank when, from behind a stone wall, the Chasseurs Britanniques opened a robust volley fire at close range that checked and unnerved the dragoons; they fell back. A similar attempt on the 51st Foot met with the same fate. Private Wheeler of the 51st recalled the effect of the volleys: 'For a moment the smoke hindered us from seeing the effect of our fire, but we soon saw plenty of horses and men stretched not so many yards from us.' The French cavalry retreated to regroup.

Craufurd's Light Division was now arriving to the rear of Houston's 7th Division. Houston moved his division further to the northwest to cover a possible flanking manoeuvre. The Light Division with the remnants of the British dragoons and light cavalry now barred the way of the French troopers. The British and Portuguese light infantry was formed into squares with the cavalry and a few field guns in between.

The French infantry and artillery was brought up to attack the Light Division, and soon, some 15 guns were on the field. The British cavalry troopers repeatedly charged the French guns, preventing their effective use against the Allied infantry packed into compact squares. Craufurd was now ordered to retreat and join the 1st Division to complete Wellington's line. This was achieved with the pursuing French cavalry close behind.

During this retreat occurred a most singular incident when Captain Norman Ramsay's two guns of Bull's troop of the Royal Horse Artillery were overtaken and surrounded by the pursuing French cavalry. They had fallen behind as they had repeatedly halted to discharge a shot or two to slow the pursuit. What happened next is best told in the stirring words of William Napier's history of the war which immortalised this event: *... a great commotion was observed amongst the French squadrons; men and officers* [of the French cavalry] *closed in confusion towards one point where a thick dust was rising, and where loud cries and sparkling of blades and flashing of pistols indicated some extraordinary occurrence. Suddenly the multitude was violently agitated, an English shout arose, the mass was rent assunder, and Norman Ramsay burst forth at the head of his battery* [actually two guns], *his horses breathing fire and stretching like greyhounds along the plain, his guns bounding like things of no weight; and the mounted gunners in close and compact order protecting the rear.*[21] As Ramsay's horse artillerymen were galloping desperately towards the British line, a squadron of the 14th Light Dragoons and a squadron of the 1st Royal Dragoons, seeing the guns in danger, turned back and charged the pursuing French cavalry which allowed Ramsay to reach the 1st Division safely amidst the cheers of its infantrymen, who had witnessed the whole incident.

The French were more fortunate a little further west. There, a piquet from Stopford's Foot Guards Brigade in Spencer's 1st Division formed a small square to resist the oncoming French cavalry. The square easily beat off the rather disorganized charge by the French troopers. Unfortunately, their commander, Lieutenant-Colonel George Hill of the Scots Guards, then ordered his men into an extended skirmish line again. At that point came a second charge made by the 13th Chasseurs à cheval that broke through three companies and cut down some 70 men in a matter of minutes, taking Hill and 20 others prisoner. The rest of the guards piquet banded together and resisted the onslaught as best it could until relieved by a troop of the 1st Royal Dragoons and a squadron of the 14th Light Dragoons. By that time, the Guards had suffered about 100 casualties.[22]

Wellington's New Line Stands Firm

These episodes were only two of several attacks made by the French cavalry on Wellington's southern flank, but the new Allied position was obviously strong. Montbrun now felt that the already hard-hit 1st Division was ripe for an all-out general charge, which, if carried out by a strong body of attacking cavalry, had a good chance of piercing the Allied line. Behind his dragoons and light cavalrymen was Lepic's Brigade – a reserve of some 881 officers and troopers of the Imperial Guard cavalry. Added to his men, these elite horsemen would form a force of some 3,500 cavalry to hurl at Spencer's 1st Division. The French infantry of Loison's 6th Corps would follow as soon as a breach had been made. Montbrun called on Lepic to bring his Guard cavalry forward, but to Monbrun's mortification, Lepic answered that he could not as only Marshal Bessières had the power

OVERLEAF
The main French attack was a frontal assault on the village of Fuentes de Oñoro, which met determined resistance from the British garrison of 24th Foot, 71st Highland Light Infantry and 79th Highlanders. A second massive assault by 18 companies of elite French grenadiers led to desperate fighting in the village and was only defeated by the timely arrival of the British light infantry companies and the 6th Portuguese Cazadores. The French now threw in two more divisions and the Allies retreated. Wellington then gave permission for Mackinnon's Brigade of Picton's 3rd Division to charge. Picton himself ordered this business must be done with cold steel.' The bayonet charge by the 45th, 74th and 88th, supported by the surviving defenders, eventually drove the French out after a desperate struggle amid streets choked with dead and wounded. Patrice Courcelle)

81

to authorise the deployment of his cavalry. A frantic search began for Bessières, who could have been anywhere on the battlefield. He was eventually found near Pezzo Bello, but by this time Monbrun's opportunity had passed as the 1st and 7th divisions and the Light Division had consolidated their positions. As Kinkaid of the 95th Rifles put it, the French that did approach 'did not seem to like our looks, as we [the Light Division] occupied a low ridge of broken rocks, against which even a rat could scarcely have hoped to advance alive.'

French accounts largely blame this blunder for the failure of their army at Fuentes de Oñoro. However, as British and Portuguese historians point out, it was far from certain that the French cavalry – Imperial Guard or not – would have broken through the British and Portuguese regiments. The 3,500 French troopers would have attacked a force four times their number. British troops were arguably the hardest to break with cavalry charges and their firepower was acknowledged as the deadliest in Europe. As the French were learning, the new Portuguese army was proving as tough and deadly on the battlefield as the British. It is impossible to know what the outcome of the charge would have been, but the strong suspicion must be that the Allied troops would have repulsed Monbrun's and Lepic's cavalry.

FRENCH ATTACKS ON THE VILLAGE

The great French cavalry attacks to the south had driven the British back to a new defence line that was actually less extended than their initial positions. This new line continued to protect the southern flank so that Masséna's troops could not relieve Almeida. The bulk of Wellington's army, mostly deployed behind Fuentes de Oñoro still had to be vanquished if the French were to prevail. Masséna ordered six divisions to attack the village and its immediate area across a 1.5-km front. This was a powerful attack force, but the target was a formidable defensive position. The low stone houses, narrow winding streets and the hills just behind it were ideal spots in which the Anglo-Portuguese defenders could dig in.

On the plateau behind the village further west was Spencer's 1st Division, then Picton's 3rd Division and Ashworth's Portuguese Brigade. In the village were the 1/71st Foot and 1/79th Foot with the 2/24th Foot on the hill just behind and ready to reinforce the two Highland battalions within minutes. Craufurd's Light Division had been withdrawn to form the reserve. Wellington, who enjoyed superiority in artillery, had also concentrated six batteries in the area. When the French artillery posted to the northeast of Fuentes de Oñoro opened up to 'soften up' the area for the attack, the Anglo-Portuguese batteries answered with such potent counter-battery fire that the fire of the French gunners soon became ineffective.

The French cavalry had been in action to the southwest for about two hours (since dawn) when Masséna, saw in the distance what was apparently his troopers sweeping all before them and ordered the assault on Fuentes de Oñoro. The attack was launched by the 4,200 men of Ferey's Division of 6th Corps, which was holding the few houses east of the small Dos Casas River. The French were initially successful, driving the 71st and 79th back about halfway into the village but the assault was checked by the arrival of the 24th Foot. To support the attack, General Drouet called upon his shock troops – three battalions made up of 18 companies of elite grenadiers drawn from both Divisions of his 9th Corps. Wearing their tall bearskin caps, these grenadiers now pushed into the village and renewed the attack, driving the three British battalions back towards the church at the foot of the hill. Wellington, seeing the increased pressure on this critical point, ordered the light companies – the same that had fought in the village two days earlier – to reinforce the men in the village. They were followed by the entire 6th Cazadores. A ferocious struggle ensued in the village's streets with no clear advantage to either side.

To break the deadlock, General Drouet decided to commit the 10,000 men from Conroux's and Clarapède's divisions for a final sweep through the village and up to the plateau so as to smash Wellington's centre. As many as ten French battalions – about 6,000 men – charged into Fuentes de Oñoro to assist their grenadier comrades. They ran through lanes already choked with the dead and wounded. The British and Portuguese soldiers fought back fiercely but had to retreat in face of superior numbers. The French 9th Light Infantry got past the little church and to the foot of the hill behind it. Just beyond was Mackinnon's Brigade of about 1,800 men made up of the 1/45th, 74th and 1/88th from Picton's 3rd Division. Sir Edward Packenham was sent to Wellington by Mackinnon to request permission to charge the French.

Wellington perceived that this was the decisive moment and immediately granted Mackinnon's Brigade permission to charge down into the village. 'We'll waste no powder' Picton said grimly, 'this business must be done with cold steel.' A few minutes later, the 1/88th charged down the hill, meeting the French 4/9th Light Infantry in a terrible clash by the church, face to face in a desperate struggle mostly with the bayonet – a street battle of heroic intensity until the French light infantrymen began to give way. The 74th charged down another street and also started driving back the French infantrymen while the exhausted Highlanders and Allied light infantry companies rallied to support the counter-attack. The tide of men surged through the streets in one of the few instances during the Peninsular War when the bayonet was used in a general engagement. The French retreated at every point and fell back across the river to its eastern bank where they halted.

The final, massive assault of the French 9th Corps had been repulsed by the Anglo-Portuguese with much slaughter, and the battle ended at about 2.00pm. The 9th Corps had lost over 800 men and Ferey's Division some 400 so that French casualties were in excess of 1,200 men. The 74th and 88th lost only 116 men while the 24th, the light companies and 6th Cazadores reported 160 casualties. After the shooting had died down, Picton encountered some men of the 88th and told them 'Well done 88th!' to which some answered 'Are we the greatest blackguards of the army now?' alluding to his former comments on the regiment. 'No, no, you are brave and gallant soldiers. This day redeemed your character.'[23]

Allied casualties suffered during the day amounted to 1,452 officers and men of which 192 were killed, 958 wounded and 255 taken prisoners. The French had 2,192 casualties of which 267 were killed,

1,878 wounded and 47 taken prisoners. Most of the French artillery's guns were put out of action by the Allied guns.

The final event of the campaign concerned the French garrison stranded in the fortress of Almeida. As the French army withdrew into Spain, Masséna sent messengers to Almeida with instructions to abandon the place and try to escape undetected. Two of the three messengers were disguised as peasants but were caught and shot as spies.

The southwestern battery at the fortress of Almeida. Its French garrison managed to slip out in May 1811. (Photo: RC)

The third messenger remained in uniform and got through to Brigadier-General Antoine-François Brenier, governor of Almeida. The place was surrounded by Pack's Portuguese Brigade until 10 May, when it was relieved by Campbell's 6th Division. Meanwhile, in the city, the French spiked guns and placed mines to ruin the fortifications. On the night of 10/11 May, Brenier and his 1,300 men slipped out quietly in two columns. They ran into piquets of the 1st Portuguese Infantry and the 2nd Foot which were quickly scattered. Just at that moment, tremendous explosions rocked Almeida, attracting the attention of the Allies so that Brenier and his men slipped through more British troops after some fighting and joined Masséna's army. It was a setback for Wellington, who was very upset. Neither Generals Campbell or Erskine had deployed their troops in a tight enough noose around the city. The French lost about 350 men in the fighting but, in Wellington's opinion, it was a disgrace that any should have escaped at all.

Nevertheless, the last of the French troops had finally left Portugal. A few hours before, on 11 May, Marshal Marmont arrived to replace Masséna.

---

20 The 17 light companies were drawn from the 2/24th, 2/42nd, 1/45th, 1/50th, 1/71st, 74th, 1/79th, 2/83rd, 1/88th, 2/88th, 1/92nd, 94th, the 1st, 2nd, 5th and 7th line battalions of the King's German Legion, the 9th and 21st Portuguese infantry.

21 William F.P. Napier, *History of the War in the Peninsula and in Southern France*, Vol. II, book XII. The event inspired a number of paintings, several of which appear in this book.

22 The French accounts of this success are rather quaint. Fririon mentioned that '300 Hussars [!] of the English Royal Guards' had been captured. A. Hugo's *France Militaire*, IV, was even better, stating that Monbrun's charge on the 'English Royal Grenadiers' had broken through and sabred their two squares and taken '1,200 prisoners, but only could bring part of them back'...!

23 As quoted in Arthur Griffiths, *The Wellington Memorial* (London, 1897), p.330. The 88th and 74th who charged with the bayonet suffered amazingly few fatalities. The 1/88th had one officer and one private killed, the 74th had one officer and two privates killed. The wounded consisted of two officers and 47 men of the 1/88th, two officers and 54 men of the 74th (Oman, IV).

AFTERMATH

The third and final French invasion of Portugal thus ended, as had the others, in failure for Napoleon's armies. Portugal was liberated and its fine army won many more victories fighting alongside their British comrades until the struggle ended with Napoleon's abdication in 1814.

Their homeland, however, was ravaged. Portugal had been a relatively wealthy country in the 18th century, but the effects of the French invasions on the country's economy were disastrous. The worst scenario, the starvation of countless refugees behind the Lines of Torres Vedras, had been averted thanks to stocks of food previously brought

ARMIES IN PORTUGAL AND SPAIN FROM JUNE 1811

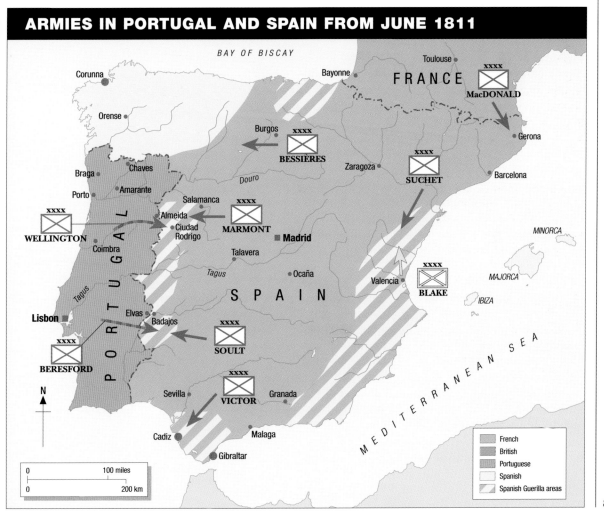

into Lisbon or sent from Britain. To alleviate the misery, the British Parliament voted £100,000 in assistance, and this was nearly matched by £94,000 raised by public appeals for aid for the Portuguese civilians. Another two million *cruzados* were sent from Brazil. As welcome as they were, such sums – huge by the monetary standards of the day – could only give relief and not even begin to address the issue of reconstruction. Tens of thousands of farms were in ruins. Countless businesses were in ashes. In the autumn of 1811, the Portuguese government compiled surveys which contained stunning figures on the extent of the devastation. Towns such as Castelo Branco, Crato, Aveiro and Pinhel rated a '1', which meant they were practically in ruins. The bill was estimated at a staggering forty million *reis*. Even in towns such as Leiria and Pombal rated with a '3', which meant they had relatively minor property damage, the figures were tragic. What capital that had not been seized by the French had gone to Brazil or to other lands promising high returns on investments. Certainly, prospects for a reasonable return were poor in Portugal where part of the business infrastructure had been shattered. Portugal's trade and commerce had decreased by about two-thirds at the war's end and did not improve substantially in the following years. The country's political and social structure was consequently much affected.

But the human cost was even higher. The first and second French invasions had included enough examples of massacres and outrages by the French troops. The 1810–11 invasion was, if anything, even worse. Personal memoirs and surveys made afterwards chronicle atrocities against the weak and defenceless that make many modern outrages seem to pale by comparison. True, a few French soldiers met unpleasant ends at the hands of crazed peasants but this, in contrast to what went on in Spain, was exceptional in Portugal. Indeed, after reading of the horrors they suffered, one wonders how the Portuguese managed to remain civilised until one realises that, like the British, they sought a military victory rather than a blood bath of vengeance. And yet, after this third invasion, cities that had been occupied by the French were depopulated. Before the 1810 invasion, the population of Leiria was some 48,000 souls. In late 1811, it was only 16,000. Some 32,000 of its inhabitants had vanished. Pombal declined from a population of 7,000 to 1,800. And the list went on. The total number of dead or missing civilians came to an incredible 200,000 people.[24]

That the British were able to open a significant front against the French in the Peninsula was very much due to the sacrifice and indomitable spirit of the Portuguese people and the Portuguese army. Equally, the Portuguese would not ultimately have been liberated from the French nor developed an army that could stand up to Napoleon's troops, had it not been for the outstanding British help in funding, supplying and training the reborn Portuguese army. With a leader such as Wellington, British and Portuguese soldiers were now ready to march into Spain and challenge the French grip on that suffering nation.

---

24 The figures on aid, damage and population losses are given in detail in Luz Soriano, III.

THE BATTLEFIELDS TODAY

The fortifications built in 1809–10 in and around Lisbon have often been the victims of urban development in the last two centuries. The third Line of Torres Vedras protecting the possible embarkation point at Sao Juliao is now totally built over. Lisbon itself is certainly a delight to visit, and a climb to the castle of St. George dominating the city's centre gives an excellent view of the city's strategic position and of the River Tagus. From the famous Tower of Belem and westwards following the shore to Cascaes and beyond, there are many seacoast forts still standing that were garrisoned at the time of the Napoleonic wars. The second Line of Torres Vedras at the level of Mafra is also much overrun by the growing suburbs of Lisbon. The first Line of Torres Vedras is also rapidly being swamped but there are still substantial remnants to see. The town of Torres Vedras has grown extensively since 1810 but is a pleasant place to stay and its small medieval castle, which formed one of the strongpoints in the line, makes an interesting visit. Torres Vedras also has a tall obelisk monument dedicated to the memory of the Anglo-Portuguese army and of the lines. Driving down various country roads will bring one to other places, such as Sobral and Pero Negro, still a small village with the mansion where Wellington had his HQ. On a hill just north of the house are what appear to be the remains of a foundation, which may have been for the telegraph station on its summit.

Heading north, Santarem on the Tagus River has expanded greatly as have most other towns. If one ventures as far as Coimbra, standing by the river Mondego at the city centre will put you in the same spot as Trant and the Portuguese levies as they watched the French across the river. Travelling east, one eventually reaches the Spanish border. The fortress of Almeida simply must be seen as its isolation has ensured its preservation. Not far to the east is the ruined Spanish fort of La Concepcion. There are really two villages of Fuentes de Oñoro. The one on the main highway is a modern border services town with all the concomitant conveniences. The village where the battle occurred is about a kilometre south along a small road. It is still a small, humble hamlet with low houses of stone, much as in 1810. Next to the small church is a simple monument to the battle erected on the scene of the desperate fighting that occurred there nearly two centuries ago, ending Napoleon's dream of total Iberian domination.

ORDERS OF BATTLE

Wellington's Allied Army, Lines of Torres Vedras, early November 1810

BRITISH ARMY
Cavalry:
Cavalry Division (Lieutenant-General Sir Stapleton Cotton): 2,833 officers and men
De Grey's Brigade: 3rd Dragoon Guards and 4th Dragoons, 804
Slade's Brigade: 1st Dragoons and 14th Light Dragoons, 808
Anson's Brigade: 16th Light Dragoons and 1st Hussars King's German Legion, 000
Unbrigaded: 13th Light Dragoons, 323

Infantry:
1st Division (Lieutenant-General Sir Brent Spencer): 6,948 officers and men
Stopford's Brigade: 1/2nd Coldstream Guards, 1/3rd Scots Guards, 5/60th Foot [Rifles] (1 coy), 1,685
Nightingale's Brigade: 2/24th Foot, 2 /42nd Foot, 1/79th Foot, 5/60th Foot [Rifles] (1 coy), 1,539
Howard's Brigade: 1/50th Foot, 1/71st Foot, 1/92nd Foot, 3/95th Rifles (1 coy), 2,043
Löwe's Brigade: 1st, 2nd, 5th and 7th Line Battalions and a light company of the King's German Legion, 1,681

2nd Division (General Rowland Hill): 5,251 officers and men
Colborne's Brigade: 1/3rd Foot, 2/31st Foot, 2/48th, 2/66th, 5/60th Foot [Rifles] (1 coy), 2,105
Houghtons's Brigade: 29th Foot, 1/48th Foot, 1/57th Foot, 5/60th Foot [Rifles] (1 coy), 1,657
Lumley's Brigade: 2/28th Foot, 2/34th Foot, 2/39th Foot, 5/60th Foot [Rifles] (1 coy), 1,489

3rd Division (Major-General Thomas Picton): 3,336 officers and men
1st Brigade Colonel Mackinnon: 74th Foot, 1/88th Foot, 1/45th Foot, 5/60th Foot [Rifles] (3 coys), 1,681
2nd Brigade (Major-General Colville): 2/5th Foot, 2/83rd Foot, 94th Foot, 5/60th Foot [Rifles] (3 coys), 1,655

4th Division (Major-General Lowry Cole), 4,792 officers and men
Kemmis's Brigade: 2/27th Foot, 1/40th Foot, 1/97th Foot, 5/60th Foot [Rifles] (1 coy), 2,572
Packenham's Brigade: 1/7th Foot, 1/61st Foot, Brunswick-Oels Jägers, 2,220

5th Division (Major-General James Leith): 3,229 officers and men
Hay's Brigade: 3/1st Foot, 1/9th Foot, 2/38th Foot, 2,047
Dunlop's Brigade: 2/30th Foot, 3/44th Foot, 1,182

6th Division (Major-General Alexander Campbell): 1,948 officers and men
Only one brigade: 2/7th Foot, 1/11th Foot, 2/53rd Foot, 5/60th Foot [Rifles] (1 coy), 1,948

Light Division (Major-General Robert Craufurd): 2,765 officers and men
Beckwith's Brigade: I/43rd Foot and companies of the 1 and 2/95th Rifles, 1,948
2nd Brigade: 1/52nd Foot and companies of the 1/95th Rifles, 1,282

Infantry unattached to any division: 938 officers and men
2/58th Foot, 2/88th Foot, King's German Legion (1 coy), 938

Artillery:
Royal Horse Artillery, 322
Royal Artillery, 845
King's German Legion Artillery, 347

Royal Engineers and artificers, 43
Wagon Train, 422
Royal Staff Corps, 40

Total Effective British Army Forces at the Lines of Torres Vedras: 34,059 including 1,908 officers. (There were a further 9,213 men in hospitals and 2,628 detached who are not counted for a grant total of 45,900.) During the fall of 1810, at Wellington's suggestion, a battalion of 500 Royal Marines and a body of 500 sailors under naval officers were landed from Admiral Berkeley's Royal Navy squadron in the Tagus River. The 'superb body of Marines' seen by Napier were on duty guarding the third ultimate inner line surrounding Fort Sao Juliao. The sailors were sent to man a flotilla of armed boats at Almeirim that kept an eye on the French just below Santarem. There were also a few posted in the Lisbon area such as some Chasseurs Britanniques at Belem.

PORTUGUESE ARMY
Infantry:
Pack's Brigade: 1st and 16th Line, 4th Cazadores, 2,267
Fonseca's Brigade: 2nd and 14th Line, 2,414
Spry's Brigade (in Leith's 5th Division): 3rd and 15th Line, 2,163
Archibald Cambell's Brigade: 4th and 10th Line, 2,407
A. Campbell's Brigade: 6th and 18th Line, 6th Cazadores, 2,442
Coleman's Brigade: 7th and 19th Line, 2nd Cazadores, 2,196
Eben's Brigade (in Alexander Campbell's 6th Divison): 8th Line and Loyal Lusitanian Legion, 2,083
Sutton's Brigade (part of Picton's 3rd Division): 9th and 21st Line, 1,961
Harvey's then Collin's Brigade (part of Cole's 4th Division): 11th and 23rd Line, 2,535
1st and 3rd Cazadores (part of the Light Division), 964
12th Line (attached to Frederico Lecor's Division), 1,213

Cavalry:
Fane's Cavalry Division: 1st, 4th, 7th and 10th regiments, 1,193

Artillery:
1st, 2nd and 4th regiments (nine batteries and garrisons in forts), 1,710

Total Effective Portuguese Regular Army: 25,530 including officers. (3,011 men sick and detached are not counted.)

Militia and Embodied Ordenanza:
Lecor's Division (at Alhandra forts): Santarem, Idanha, Castelo Branco, Covilhao and Feira militia regiments, 2,616
At Bucelas forts: Lisbon (Thermo), Tomar and Torres Vedras militia regiments, 1,907
At the Sobral forts: Atiradores Nacionaes Ordenanza, 761
Lisbon Oriental, Lisbon Occidental, Setubal and Alcaçer militia regiments, 2,231
At the Mafra forts: Viseu Militia Regiment, 691
Ordenanza and militia volunteers artillery, 1,882

Total Effective Portuguese Militia and Ordenanza: 10,088 including officers. (1,267 men sick and detached are not counted.)

Total Effective Portuguese Army, Militia and Ordenanza at the Lines of Torres Vedras: 35,618 including officers.

There were also about 6,740 men at the depots of regular and militia regiments behind the lines and the training depot at the Fortress of Peniche that would have included 2,000–3,000 largely untrained men. The total also does not include the units which were posted in Lisbon and at the forts at the mouth of the Tagus such as at Belem and Almada.

SPANISH ARMY
(Part of General José Caro Marquis La Romana's Army of Estramadura)

Vanguard Division (General La Carrera)
1 and 2nd Bns/Principe Regiment, 1st Catalonia Regiment, 2nd Catalonia Regiment and one battalion of the Vittoria Regiment, about 2,500

2nd Division (General Carlos O'Donnell)
Zamora, Rey, Toledo, Hibernia, Princesa and 2nd Sevilla regiments, about 5,500

Total Effective Spanish Army at the Lines of Torres Vedras: about 8,000 including officers.

Grand Total of British, Portuguese and Spanish troops at the Lines of Torres Vedras: 77,677 officers and men.

The Portuguese Army, January 1811

January 1811 'Abstract of the Portuguese Forces':
Cavalry — 5,636 rank and file, 4,119 horses.
Infantry — 36,095 rank and file, including 1,626 recruits and 186 men absent without leave.
Artillery — 3,986 rank and file.
Militia — 44,356 rank and file, including 5,596 absent without leave. Return dated 21 November 1810.
Recapitulation:
Regular troops — 45,717.
Police Corps — 1,207.
Militia — 44,356.
Total: 91,280.
(Public Records Office, Foreign Office 63/160)

The Anglo-Portuguese Army at Fuentes de Oñoro, 3–5 May 1811

Officer Commanding:
Lieutenant-General Arthur, Viscount Wellington

Cavalry Division (Lieutenant-General Sir Stapleton Cotton): 1,854
1st Brigade (Major-General John Slade)
1st Dragoons, 388
14th Light Dragoons, 378
2nd Brigade (Lieutenant-Colonel F. von Arentschild)
16th Light Dragoons, 362
1st Hussars, King's German Legion, 414
3rd Brigade (Brigadier-General de Barbacena)
4th Portuguese Cavalry, 104
10th Portuguese Cavalry, 208

Infantry:
1st Division (Lieutenant-General Sir Brent Spencer): 7,565
1st Brigade (Colonel E. Stopford)
1/2nd Coldstream Guards, 940
1/3rd Scots Guards, 959
5/60th Foot [Rifles] (1 coy), 44
2nd Brigade (Major-General M. Nightingall)
2/24th Foot, 371
2 /42nd Foot, 445
1/79th Foot, 922
5/60th Foot [Rifles] (1 coy), 36
3rd Brigade (Major-General Howard)
1/50th Foot, 597
1/71st Foot, 497
1/92nd Foot, 764
3/95th Rifles (1 coy) 76
4th Brigade (Major-General Seigismund Baron von Löwe)

1st Line Bn. King's German Legion, 512
2nd Line Bn. King's German Legion, 484
5th Line Bn. King's German Legion, 422
7th Line Bn. King's German Legion, 410
Light Bn. King's German Legion (2 companies), 86

3rd Division (Major-General Thomea Picton): 5,480
1st Brigade Colonel Henry Mackinnon
74th Foot, 485
1/88th Foot, 467
1/45th Foot, 508
5/60th Foot [Rifles] (3 coys), 183
2nd Brigade (Major-General Charles Colville)
2/5th Foot, 504
2/83rd Foot, 460
2/88th Foot, 687
94th Foot, 536
3rd Brigade (Colonel Manly Power)
9th Portuguese Infantry, 910
21th Portuguese Infantry, 740

5th Division (Major-General Sir William Erskine): 5,158
1st Brigade (Brigadier-General Andrew Hay)
3/1st Foot, 672
1/9th Foot, 627
2/38th Foot, 402
Brunswick-Oels (1 coy), 69
2nd Brigade (Major-General Dunlop)
1/4th Foot, 612
2/30th Foot, 507
3/44th Foot, 437
Brunswick-Oels (1 coy), 68
3rd Brigade (Brigadier-General William Spry)
3rd Portuguese Infantry, 724
15th Portuguese Infantry, 556
8th Cazadores, 484

6th Division (Major-General Alexander Campbell): 5,250
1st Brigade (Colonel Hulse)
1/11th Foot, 837
2/53rd Foot, 459
1/61st Foot, 697
5/60th Foot [Rifles] (1 coy), 48
2nd Brigade (Colonel Burne)
1/36th Foot, 514
2nd Foot, 558
3rd Brigade (Colonel Madden)
8th Portuguese Infantry, 915
12th Portuguese Infantry, 1,222

7th Division (Major-General William Houston)
1st Brigade (Major-General Sontag)
2/51st Foot, 590
85th Foot, 387
Chasseurs Britanniques, 839
Brunswick-Oels (8 companies), 593
2nd Brigade (Brigadier-General Doyle)
7th Portuguese Infantry, 713
19th Portuguese Infantry, 1,024
2nd Cazadores, 442

Light Division (Brigadier-General Robert Craufurd): 3,815
1st Brigade, (Lieutenant-Colonel T.S. Beckwith)
I/43rd Foot, 754
1/95th Rifles (4 coys), 354
2/95th Rifles (1 coy), 76
3rd Cazadores 447
2nd Brigade (Colonel G. Drummond)
1/52nd Foot, 835
2/52nd Foot, 542
1/95th Rifles (4 coys), 357
1st Cazadores, 450

Portuguese Independent Brigade (Colonel Charles Ashworth)
6th Portuguese Infantry, 713
18th Portuguese Infantry, 1,130
6th Cazadores, 423

Artillery
R. Bull's Troop, Royal Horse Artillery
H.D. Ross's Troop, Royal Horse Artillery
R. Lawson's Company, Royal Artillery
G. Thompson's Company, Royal Artillery
F.A. de Sequerra's Battery, 2nd Portuguese Artillery
J. de Preto's Battery, 1st Portuguese Artillery
P. de Rozziere's Battery, 1st Portuguese Artillery
J.C. Rosado's Battery 2nd Portuguese Artillery

The French Army at Fuentes de Oñoro, 3–5 May 1811

THE FRENCH ARMY OF PORTUGAL

Officer Commanding:
Marshal André Masséna, Prince of Essling, Duke of Rivoli

2nd Corps – General Jean-Louis Reynier
1st Division: Pierre Merle
Brigade Sarrut
1, 2 & 3/2nd Light Infantry 55 officers, 1,812 men
1, 2 & 3/36th Line Infantry 55 officers, 1,595 men
Brigade Graindorge
1, 2 & 3/4th Light Infantry 61 officers, 1,313 men
Division Merle total 171 officers, 4,720 men

2nd Division Etienne Heudelet
Brigade Godard
1, 2 &3/17th Light Infantry 58 officers, 1,166 men
1, 2 & 3/70th Line Infantry 52 officers, 1,026 men
Brigade Arnaud
1, 2 & 3/31st Light Infantry 55 officers, 1,528 men
1, 2 & 3/47th Line Infantry 60 officers, 1,546 men
Division Heudelet total 225 officers, 5,266 men

Cavalry Brigade:
1st Hussars 9 officers, 94 men
22nd Chasseurs à cheval 27 officers, 336 men
8th Dragons 13 officers, 203 men

Total of 2nd Corps: 11,064

6th Corps – Major-General Jean-Baptiste Loison
1st Division: Jean-Gabriel Marchand
Brigade Maucune
1, 2 & 4/6th Light Infantry 43 officers, 1,202 men
1, 2 & 4/69th Line Infantry 54 officers, 1,537 men
Brigade Jean Chemineau
1, 2 & 3/39th Light Infantry 37 officers, 1,150 men
1, 2 & 3/76th Line Infantry 39 officers, 1,247 men
Division Marchand total 214 officers, 5,658 men

2nd Division: Julien Mermet
Brigade Ménard
1, 2 & 4/25th Light Infantry 67 officers, 1,800 men
1, 2 & 4/27th Line Infantry 57 officers, 1,763 men
Brigade Taupin
1, 2 & 4/50th Line Infantry 57 officers, 1,356 men
1, 2 & 4/59th Line Infantry 53 officers, 1,549 men
Division Mermet total 234 officers, 6,468 men

3rd Division: Claude-François Ferey
4, 5 & 6/26th Line Infantry 57 officers, 958 men
Légion du Midi (1 bn) 16 officers, 369 men
Légion Hanovrienne (1 bn) 19 officers, 412 men
4, 5 & 6/66th Line Infantry 63 officers, 1,307 men
4 & 6/82nd Line Infantry 44 officers, 987 men
Division Ferey total 199 officers, 4,033 men

Cavalry Brigade: Etienne Lamotte
3rd Hussars 15 officers, 152 men
15th Chasseurs à cheval 13 officers, 157 men
Cavalry Brigade Lamotte total 25 officers, 309 men

Total of 6th Corps 17,140

8th Corps – General Andoche Junot, Duke of Abrantes
1st Division: Bertrand Clausel: Absent guarding communications.

2nd Division: Jean-Baptiste Solignac
1, 2 & 3/15th Line Infantry 55 officers, 1,206 men
1, 2 & 3/86th Line Infantry 60 officers, 1,440 men
1, 2 & 4/65th Line Infantry 51 officers, 1,512 men
Régiment Irlandais (Irish Regiment, 1 bn) 18 officers, 372 men
Division Solignac total 184 officers, 4,530 men

Total of 8th Corps 4,714

9th Corps – General of Division Jean-Baptiste Drouet, Count d'Erlon
Division: Michel Claparède
54th Line Infantry (1 bn) 14 officers, 270 men
21st Light Infantry (1 bn) 16 officers, 613 men
28th Light Infantry (1 bn) 17 officers, 457 men
40th Line Infantry (1 bn) 19 officers, 500 men
63rd Line Infantry (1 bn) 19 officers, 499 men
88th Line Infantry (1 bn) 18 officers, 635 men
64th Line Infantry (1 bn) 20 officers, 563 men
100th Line Infantry (1 bn) 15 officers, 499 men
103rd Line Infantry (1 bn) 18 officers, 524 men
Division Claparède total 154 officiers, 4,560 men

Division: Nicolas Conroux
16th Light Infantry (1 bn) 16 officers, 593 men
9th Light Infantry (1 bn) 21 officers, 739 men
27th Light Infantry (1 bn) 19 officers, 648 men
8th Line Infantry (1 bn) 17 officers, 599 men
24th Line Infantry (1 bn) 17 officers, 625 men
45th Line Infantry (1 bn) 18 officers, 427 men
94th Line Infantry (1 bn) 18 officers, 678 men
95th Line Infantry (1 bn) 20 officers, 594 men
96th Line Infantry (1 bn) 18 officers, 521 men
Division Conroux total 164 officers, 5,424 men

Fournier's Cavalry Brigade:
7th Chasseurs à cheval 12 officers, 270 men
13th Chasseurs à cheval 20 officers, 250 men
20th Chasseurs à cheval 16 officers, 226 men
Fournier's Cavalry Brigade total 48 officers, 746 men

Total of 9th Corps 11,098

Reserve of Cavalry: General of Division Louis-Pierre Montbrun
Brigade Cavrois:
3rd Dragoons 12 officers, 81 men
6th Dragoons 12 officers, 126 men
15th Dragoons 11 officers, 219 men
Brigade Ornano
6th Dragoons 21 officers, 305 men
11th Dragoons 11 officers, 167 men
25th Dragoons 22 officers, 200 men
Reserve of Cavalry total 89 officers, 1,187 men

Artillery: 20 officers, 410
Engineers, Sappers, Train, etc.: 17 officers, 880 men

Total Army of Portugal 1,795 officers, 44,919 men

The French Army of the North

Officer Commanding:
Marshal Jean-Baptiste Bessières, Duke of Istria

Louis Lepic's Brigade of Imperial Guard Cavalry:
Polish Lancers 30 officers, 340 men
Chasseurs à cheval 13 officers, 222 men
Grenadiers à cheval 12 officers, 185 men
Mamelukes 10 officers, 69 men
Lepic's Brigade total 65 officers, 816 men

Pierre Wathier's Light Cavalry Brigade:
11th Chasseurs à cheval 11 officers, 220 men
12th Chasseurs à cheval 9 officers, 172 men
24th Chasseurs à cheval 7 officers, 193 men
5th Hussars 7 officers, 165 men
Wathier's Brigade total 34 officers, 750 men

Artillery (one battery): 3 officers, 70 men

Total Army of the North 102 officers, 1,636 men
Total Army of Portugal 1,795 officers, 44,919 men

Grand total 1,897 officers, 46,555 men = 48,452 all ranks

Mobilized Militias in Portugal

During the 1810–11 French invasion, the following Portuguese militia
regiments or related units were mobilised. Most were released from
active service in late 1811 and early 1812. Those kept on duty in 1812
are noted.

Militia Regiments:
Arganil (kept on duty in 1812)
Arouca
Alcacer (kept on duty in 1812)
Aveiro (kept on duty in 1812)
Arcos (kept on duty in 1812)
Beja (kept on duty in 1812)
Basto (kept on duty in 1812)
Braga
Barca
Barcelos
Braganza
Castello Branco
Covilha (kept on duty in 1812)
Coimbra
Chaves
Evora
Figueira
Faro
Feira
Guarda
Guimaraes
Idanha (kept on duty in 1812)
Lagos
Lamego
Louza
Leira
Lisbon Occidental [25]
Lisbon Oriental
Moncorvo
Maia
Miranda
Oliveira de Azemeis
Portalegre (kept on duty in 1812)
Porto
Peñafiel
Soure
Santarem
Setubal (kept on duty in 1812)
Tavira (kept on duty in 1812)
Tondela (kept on duty in 1812)
Trancoso (kept on duty in 1812)
Torres Vedras
Villa Vicosa (kept on duty in 1812)
Vizeu
Villa do Conde
Viana (kept on duty in 1812)
Villa Real

Volunteers:
Royal Commerce Volunteers of Lisbon (kept on duty in 1812)
Royal Commerce Volunteers of Porto (kept on duty in 1812)
Coimbra University Corps

Miscellaneous units:
Chaves Grenadier Battalion (kept on duty in 1812)
Chaves Cazadores Battalion
1st Uniao [Union] Battalion
2nd Uniao [Union] Battalion
Vianna Company (kept on duty in 1812)
Valenza Company (kept on duty in 1812)
Beira Baixa Company (kept on duty in 1812)
Beira Alta Company (kept on duty in 1812)
S. Joao da Foz Company (kept on duty in 1812)
Buarcos and Figuera garrisons (kept on duty in 1812)

Militia Artillery units:
Chaves Territorial Artillery (kept on duty in 1812)
Vila Real Artillery (kept on duty in 1812)
Braganza Artillery (kept on duty in 1812)
Lisbon Oriental Artillery
Lisbon Occidental Artillery
Moncorvo Territorial Artillery (kept on duty in 1812)
Régua Territorial Artillery (kept on duty in 1812)
Algarve Garrison Artillery (kept on duty in 1812)

Ordenanza Artillery units:
Torres Vedras Ordenanza Artillery
Sobral Ordenanza Artillery
Alhandra Ordenanza Artillery
Bucellas Ordenanza Artillery
Cabeza do Montachique Ordenanza Artillery
Mafra Ordenanza Artillery

---

25 The infantry battalions of Oriental and Occidental Lisbon were organised as
light infantry *atiradores* (sharpshooters) and eventually became known as
National Cazadores by 1814.

**Modern Fuentes de Oñoro is a border town with services for
travellers on the highway crossing into Portugal from the
east or Spain from the west. The historic village where the
battle was fought is a kilometre to the south of the modern
town. (Photo: RC)**

FURTHER READING

Sir Charles Oman's *History of the Peninsular War*, Vols. 3 and 4 (Oxford, 1908 and 1911), is still an excellent guide to the campaign. *The Dispatches of Field Marshal the Duke of Wellington* (London, 1838) and the *Supplementary Despatches, Correspondence, and Memoranda of Field Marshal Arthur Duke of Wellington* (London, 1860) are essential as published documents of the campaign. William Napier's *History of the Peninsular War* (London, 1835) should be used with caution. British participants have left valuable personal memoirs and letters that have been published and many are quoted in the text. For complete titles, see the excellent bibliographies in Paddy Griffith, ed., *History of the Penninsular War: Vol. IX, Modern Studies of the War in Spain and Portugal, 1808–1814* (London, 1999), Oman's *Wellington's Army* and the general indexes of the *Journal of the Society for Army Historical Research*. John Grehan's *The Lines of Torres Vedras* (London, 2000) and A. Norris and R. Bremner's *The Lines of Torres Vedras* (Lisbon, 1980) ably cover that subject.

The British army is well covered in Oman's *Wellington's Army* (London, 1913) and in Philip J. Haythornthwaite's *The Armies of Wellington* (London, 1994). Regimental histories of the various British regiments involved all cover their unit's participation. John Elting's *Swords Around a Throne* (New York, 1988) is one of the best works dealing with Napoleon's troops. There are few works in English on the Portuguese forces besides Andrew Halliday's *The Present State of Portugal and of the Portuguese Army* (Edinburgh, 1813) and the author's *Portuguese Army of the Napoleonic Wars* (Osprey Men-at-Arms Series, Nos. 343, 346 and 356).

There are few published French sources on this campaign. A good overview from the French perspective is in A. Hugo's *France Militaire*, Vol. 4 (Paris, 1837). Of the French memoirs, Baron Marbot's is perhaps the most revealing. Correspondence and biographies of marshals Ney and Masséna are important if focusing more on their mutual disputes than on the campaign. French statistics should be used with caution because of obvious exaggerations.

In Portuguese, essential data for the 1811 campaign is found in Simao José da Luz Soriano's *Historia da Guerra Civil … Guerra da Peninsula*, Vol. III (Lisbon 1874). Christovam Ayres de Magalhaes Sepulveda, *Historia Organica e Politica do Exercito Portugues*, Vols. XI–XIII (Coimbra, 1916–1925), has excellent documents and compilations. Claudio de Chaby's *Excerptos Historicos e Colleccao de Documentos Relativa a la Guerra Denomida da Peninsula …*, Vols. III to VI (Lisbon, 1865–82) is somewhat dated but still very useful. Ferreira Martins' *Historia do Exercito Portugues* (Lisbon, 1945) is the standard history of the army. A good overview of the army and the campaign is given in Carlos Selvagem, *Portugal Militar: Compendio de Historia Militar e Naval de Portugal* (Lisbon, 1931, reprinted 1999), a classic compilation of Portuguese military history on land and sea.

Additional sources are detailed in the footnotes.

INDEX

COMPANION SERIES FROM OSPREY

ESSENTIAL HISTORIES
Concise studies of the motives, methods and repercussions of human conflict, spanning history from ancient times to the present day. Each volume studies one major war or arena of war, providing an indispensable guide to the fighting itself, the people involved, and its lasting impact on the world around it.

MEN-AT-ARMS
The uniforms, equipment, insignia, history and organisation of the world's military forces from earliest times to the present day. Authoritative text and full-colour artwork, photographs and diagrams bring over 5000 years of history vividly to life.

ELITE
This series focuses on uniforms, equipment, insignia and unit histories in the same way as Men-at-Arms but in more extended treatments of larger subjects, also including personalities and techniques of warfare.

NEW VANGUARD
The design, development, operation and history of the machinery of warfare through the ages. Photographs, full-colour artwork and cutaway drawings support detailed examinations of the most significant mechanical innovations in the history of human conflict.

ORDER OF BATTLE
The greatest battles in history, featuring unit-by-unit examinations of the troops and their movements as well as analysis of the commanders' original objectives and actual achievements. Colour maps including a large fold-out base map, organisational diagrams and photographs help the reader to trace the course of the fighting in unprecedented detail.

WARRIOR
Insights into the daily lives of history's fighting men and women, past and present, detailing their motivation, training, tactics, weaponry and experiences. Meticulously researched narrative and full-colour artwork, photographs, and scenes of battle and daily life provide detailed accounts of the experiences of combatants through the ages.

AIRCRAFT OF THE ACES
Portraits of the elite pilots of the 20th century's major air campaigns, including unique interviews with surviving aces. Unit listings, scale plans and full-colour artwork combine with the best archival photography available to provide a detailed insight into the experience of war in the air.

COMBAT AIRCRAFT
The world's greatest military aircraft and combat units and their crews, examined in detail. Each exploration of the leading technology, men and machines of aviation history is supported by unit listings and other data, artwork, scale plans, and archival photography.

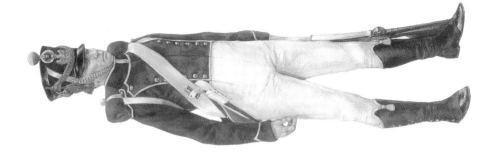 

FIND OUT MORE ABOUT OSPREY

❑ Please send me a FREE trial issue
  of Osprey Military Journal

❑ Please send me the latest listing of Osprey's publications

❑ I would like to subscribe to Osprey's e-mail newsletter

Title/rank

Name

Address

Postcode/zip   state/country

e-mail

Which book did this card come from?

❑ I am interested in military history

My preferred period of military history is _____

❑ I am interested in military aviation

My preferred period of military aviation is _____

I am interested in *(please tick all that apply)*

❑ general history   ❑ militaria   ❑ model making
❑ wargaming   ❑ re-enactment

Please send to:

USA & Canada: Osprey Direct USA, c/o Motorbooks
International, P.O. Box 1, 729 Prospect Avenue, Osceola,
WI 54020

UK, Europe and rest of world:
Osprey Direct UK, P.O. Box 140, Wellingborough, Northants,
NN8 2FA, United Kingdom

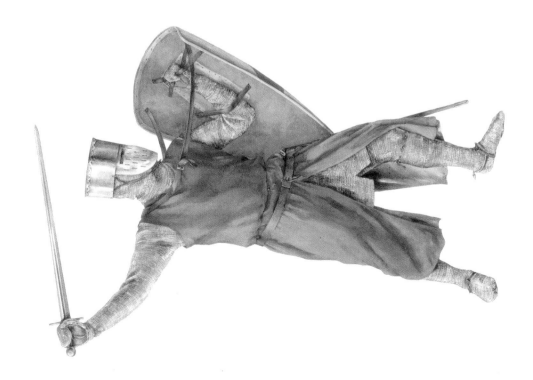

OSPREY
PUBLISHING

www.ospreypublishing.com

call our telephone hotline
for a free information pack

USA & Canada: 1-800-458-0454
UK, Europe and rest of world call:
+44 (0) 1933 443 863

Young Guardsman
Figure taken from *Warrior 22:
Imperial Guardsman 1799–1815*
Published by Osprey
Illustrated by Richard Hook

Knight, c.1190
Figure taken from *Warrior 1: Norman Knight 950 – 1204AD*
Published by Osprey
Illustrated by Christa Hook

POSTCARD